Publisher's Note

This volume is one of a planned series of books compiled from the lectures and workshops of some of the most innovative and articulate contributors to modern astrology's development. We call the series *Lectures on Modern Astrology* to stress the fact that the material included in this series will have to meet most or all of the following criteria:

- the use of clear, modern language
- a particularly sharp vision of astrology's unique value and potential
- *a person-centered focus* rather than the traditional event-oriented preoccupation with predictions (although an intelligent, *integrated* use of event potentialities and trends lies within this definition)
- providing some new contribution to the on-going development of a broad-based astrological psychology that does not merely speculate about but which actually *illuminates* human experience and behavior.

It is our belief that today much of the best material and most of the new ideas of real value are being presented—not in formal, book-length volumes—but in lectures and workshops (as well as in an occasional journal article). By providing this medium of edited transcripts in book form, we feel that some of the most vital and incisive of today's astrological thought—which heretofore has been communicated only to small groups in person and then passes into oblivion—can now be given a permanent form and a wider availability. In this way, we hope to contribute to the building of a new tradition of intelligent, in-depth astrology and to the evolving formulation of a language for *person-centered* astrology that is both accurate and appropriate for growth-oriented people.

Those who want to be notified of future volumes in this series should write us and ask to be on our mailing list.

The Outer Planets & Their Cycles

The Astrology of the Collective

Liz Greene

CRCS Publications
Post Office Box 20850
Reno, Nevada 89515
U.S.A.

Library of Congress Cataloging in Publication Data

Greene, Liz.
   The outer planets & their cycles.
     (The astrology of the collective.)

(Lectures on modern astrology series.)
   1. Astrology--Addresses, essays, lectures.
2. Planets--Miscellanea--Addresses, essays, lectures.
I. Title. II. Series.
BF1708.1.G75 1983   133.5'3   82-45633
ISBN 0-916360-17-2 (pbk.)

FIRST EDITION
INTERNATIONAL STANDARD BOOK NUMBER: 0-916360-17-2
LIBRARY OF CONGRESS CATALOG CARD NUMBER: 82-045633
Published simultaneously in the United States and Canada by:
CRCS Publications
Distributed in the United States and internationally by
CRCS Publications
(Write for current list of worldwide distributors.)
Cover Design: Image & lettering both by Rebecca Wilson
Illustrations & charts all drawn by Liz Greene

Contents

Introduction

The series of lectures which follow was first given in April 1980 as a weekend residential conference under the auspices of the Wrekin Trust, held near Bath, the old Roman spa in the county of Avon, England. The Wrekin Trust was created by Sir George Trevelyan in 1971 as a charitable foundation committed to the exploration of various aspects of spiritual and psychological knowledge. I have been fortunate to be able to offer workshops and conferences on a number of astrological themes under the umbrella of this organisation, and would like to thank both Sir George Trevelyan and Malcolm Lazarus, the programme director, for their help and support in these ventures.

Almost three years have passed between the conference and the publication of the talks. Many of the themes which I had begun to explore at that time have developed and changed, and so have world events. The main emphasis of the conference dealt with currents in the collective psyche which surface as political and religious movements and visions, both in society and in the individual, and a good deal has happened since 1980 which dates some of the material. In 1980 I was watching the then future conjunction of Saturn and Pluto in Libra with some trepidation, because on each former occasion when the conjunction has occurred in this century there has been a major outbreak of war just prior to it. At the time that I am writing this introduction, the conjunction has been within orb for many months and is approaching its exact meeting in twenty-seven degrees of Libra. An undeclared war has already occurred between Great Britain and Argentina, and another, perhaps more potentially serious, has broken out in the Middle East where Israel has busied herself rooting out the Palestinian Liberation Organisation by dismembering Lebanon. Although neither of these happenings has resulted in a global conflagration, there has nevertheless been a degree of slaughter fit for the umbrella of a Saturn-Pluto conjunction. Although much has happened both in the world and in terms of my own increased understanding of the outer planets and the energies they symbolise, the original intent of the conference remains unchanged in my mind, and has resulted in the transcription of the lectures and the publication of this book. Briefly, that intent is to try to bring a little more insight to bear on profound and powerful eruptions and shifts in the collective psyche, the matrix which Jung described so extensively in his *Collected Works* as the sea out of which all individual personality emerges.

Since the conference my training and work as a Jungian analyst have offered me rich opportunity to watch the workings of the outer planets in the dreams and ongoing life experiences of my analysands as well as my astrological clients. This direct experience of what previously had been intuitive speculation based on horoscope readings alone has confirmed my feeling that the outer planets are deeply significant representatives of the collective operating within the individual's life framework, and that they perform like a force of fate—blind, compulsive, overwhelming and often destructive—unless the ego can develop enough insight to distinguish itself from the collective currents of which it is a part. As Jung puts it in Volume 16 of the *Collected Works*, "In these circumstances the immunising of the individual against the toxin of the mass psyche is the only thing that can help." More than anyone else except perhaps the psychotherapist and the priest, the astrologer today must respond with equilibrium to the chronic terror of holocaust and apocalypse which is so widespread at present and generates so much anxiety in people's lives. It was to these themes that the Wrekin Trust conference was addressed, and the urgency which I felt then about the need for greater understanding of the outer planets among the astrological community has not decreased in the intervening three years.

As an analyst who works primarily with individuals, I am not overwhelmingly sympathetic to the belief that we can change the world to our own noble designs by shouting at everybody else from marches and picket lines about the evils of organisations and political parties, or by manufacturing grand well-meaning schemes by which spiritual enlightenment might be offered to to the blind and stupid masses. There is enough blindness and stupidity in oneself to provide occupation for a lifetime if not longer, and I am firmly on the side of Jung when he says that if there is something wrong with society then there is something wrong with the individual, and if there is something wrong with the individual then there is something wrong with me. That is the dictum by which any responsible counselor or therapist must work: if one has any hope or idealism for a better life and a better world, the place to begin is with one's own *prima materia*, the commencement of every alchemical opus and in the final analysis the only thing to which the individual has any access or, perhaps, any right. Although the material in these lectures is about larger movements in the collective, and includes interpretation of the horoscopes of various countries, it is nevertheless oriented primarily toward individual interpretation. It is the individual who in the end gives expression to collective myths and visions, and society is ultimately a conglomerate of individuals, not an abstract entity with an independent existence. The outer planets are transpersonal, that is, beyond the personal, but they reveal themselves through the psychology of individuals, that is, through you and me. For this reason I feel that if one is genuinely concerned with issues of good and evil in the world, then one will ultimately need to encounter these issues within oneself. That is the only place where any hope of resolution can be found. Projecting good and evil into countries and ideologies is a fascinating and relieving pastime, but leads nowhere except into hopelessness and despair—at present a common enough state.

Hence, there are no solutions offered in these lectures for the woes of the world, and it will be difficult for the reader to ascertain any particular political stance. In fact, no solutions of any kind are offered at all. My intention was to raise questions and help to promote individual reflection and application of what astrological insights we may have about the outer planets in our own lives. That was the purpose of the Wrekin Trust conference, and the purpose remains unchanged.

L. G.

November 1982
London

Lecture One

One of the primary reasons why I chose the particular subject of this conference is that there seems to be a tremendous amount of millenarian fear around at the present time, and I am concerned with what this might mean. I would define millenarian fear as an expectant waiting for the end of the world to come. Now there are some very good rational reasons for this, like the prodigious amount of Russian armaments on the German border, and the proliferation of nuclear weapons and nuclear power plants. If you turn on your television set or pick up a newspaper you can get extremely frightened very quickly, and it would be both dishonest and stupid to pretend that these dangers are not real. But there is also an atmosphere which I don't really think arises from these dangers alone, and which possibly makes it even more difficult to react with a sane response to critical but nevertheless poten tially manageable external situations. We stand at the end of a century and at the end of a millennium, as well as at the end of an astrological age. Very strange fantasies erupt in society at such times, which may be related to but are not caused by affairs in the outside world.

Something seems to be going on at a subterranean level which catches all of us and throws us into a state of anxiety which is above and beyond the ordinary conscious reactions we might have to things read in the newspaper. It is a sense of the advent of something, a sense of great change. If you are familiar with the predictions of psychics about the end of this century, you will know that these usually deal with tidal waves, giant earthquakes, the landing of flying saucers, the Second Coming of Christ, and the earth shifting on its polar axis. But these kinds of predictions aren't unique to us in the twentieth century. They are archetypal images of change, deep psychic change at an unconscious collective level. You can meet these images in the dreams of individuals who are undergoing profound shifts and transformations in their inner and outer lives, and you meet the same images in the mouths of prophets at the end of the millennium, whichever millennium it is. Those of us who work in the astrological field have only to open an ephemeris and look at the rather peculiar conjunctions which are approaching in the next twenty years. It isn't as though they have never happened before. But when they coincide with the end of a millennium, then people tend to panic, even astrologers who ought to know better. Someone rang me up recently, quite late at night, and said, "I understand that you're an astrologer. Is it true that all the planets will collide in 1984?" This is the sort of thing I mean. I must admit that I find it disturbing, because there is an ominous foreboding in the atmosphere that is not necessarily in line with world events. It seems to me that there is enough difficulty in trying to deal with actual facts, let alone these strange fantasies and terrors. Some of these fantasies are exaggeratedly spiritual, like the Second Coming, and some of them are exaggeratedly concrete, like a worldwide holocaust.

On the other hand, even though we can try to understand these undercurrents from a psychological point of view, it's equally useless to pretend that we are so sane and rational and perceptive that we won't react in the same way everyone else does. The collective unconscious, which is Jung's term for the deep strata of the human psyche which are common to us all, is something we don't know very much about. We know a good deal about collective consciousness, which concerns the rules and structures that society creates and by which we supposedly learn to live with and cooperate with each other. But the underground stream that runs beneath the surface of those structures—that is a mystery. We only recognise its existence when it bursts into external life, and one of the ways in which it shows itself is that an entire group or country goes berserk and you have one of those gigantic upheavals or revolutions which ends in a bloodbath. An entire nation can plunge into psychosis in the same way an individual can, and a lot of apparently very rational people disappear and become one screaming mob. You can observe a small paradigm of this at any football match. There are people who are more prone to being infected by it than others. There are people who are permeable to perhaps a greater extent than others. There are people who believe they are immune, yet who are in the greatest danger. There are people who seem to have an inherent natural connection with this world of collective unconscious psyche, and somehow find a way to live with it and mediate it. These are the artists and visionaries. Because they are familiar with it, and can offer it some kind of voice through their personal creative efforts, they are not as surprised as the rest of us when an eruption suddenly occurs in the world. I'm thinking now of William Butler

Yeats and his poem, *The Second Coming*, which was written long before the rise of Nazi Germany and was his vision of the new astrological age—a rather terrifying vision, not at all imbued with love and brotherhood. The artist and the visionary are driven by the images that rise out of that strange world, and its compulsions become their message. The line is very blurred between the artist and the psychotic, I believe because both have dealings with this realm. And there are people who actively attempt to manipulate its energies, for good or ill.

I think Adolf Hitler is a good example of someone who successfully manipulated the images of the collective unconscious for his own dubious ends. There are quite a number of gifted manipulators in the fields of politics and religion. These are issues which I think must be talked about, not only because of what lies ahead of us in the next few decades, but also so that we can look back historically at what has happened when major conjunctions and millenarian visions have occurred before, and draw some lessons from the past. This might equip us to measure better the trends that are coming up, in the same way that any of you studying individual astrology will measure your experience from the past to interpret a new horoscope in the present.

I believe we can tell a lot from the individual birth chart about permeability or receptivity to the realm of the collective unconscious. People are very different in the ways in which they experience and relate to this mysterious world, in the ways they interpret it, and in the channels through which it expresses itself in their lives. This is why one person will sense some great change coming and panic, while another will trundle along innocently enough until the roof blows up over his head.

This is ground which is not generally covered in astrology, although Jung wrote a great deal about his observations in this area. Many people feel his work on the archetypes and the collective unconscious was his greatest contribution to psychology. Most of our modern therapies deal with the individual, whether internally or in terms of his adjustment to society. That is as it should be, because there is no way to "treat" the collective through therapy. We can only explore ourselves. This is another reason why the eruptions of the collective are such a problem and such a mystery. Jung worked a great deal with myths, which he felt were the images through which the collective expressed itself culturally. I feel we must begin bringing some of this material into astrology. In earlier times, particularly during the Renaissance, astrologers did work with what they understood as the manifestations of the collective, through eclipses and great conjunctions. But their interpretations were always very literal, about wars and plagues and the deaths of kings. Now we don't consider these things very viable, and have lost a good deal of the knowledge of the Renaissance about astrological influences on political affairs. As I said earlier, I am concerned about these issues because a lot of people are very frightened, and the astrologer quite naturally gets asked first if the world is going to end. I would like to inject a slightly more hopeful note into all this millenarian terror. It isn't hope built on an idealistic or mystical belief that we are about to reach an apotheosis of human spirituality or glory. I would be fairly stupid if I believed that, given the current state of things. That might be true at Wrekin Trust conferences, but it isn't true anywhere else. Nevertheless these are tremendous, powerful, creative energies, and they don't always have to manifest in a solely destructive way. I have no answers about what to do with them, but I think it might make a difference if we could understand them a little better, and see where they are working in our individual lives.

I must apologise to the absolute beginners in the room, because we will be discussing quite a few horoscopes which you will not be able to read. It did say in the programme, however, that some basic astrological knowledge was essential for participation at the conference, so you have only yourselves to blame. You were also asked to bring your own individual charts, and hopefully if some of you have questions and would like your charts used as an illustration, we can draw them on the blackboard. There is obviously no time to give a chart reading to everybody in the group. I will also be referring to the charts of people who figure or have figured importantly through history, as vessels or mediums for the collective, ranging from the very dark ones to the very light ones. We can investigate what there is in the birth horoscope that might suggest the particular susceptibility to this realm. Some people, as I said, have a very minimal relationship with it. They aren't aware of it at all, although of course it is still part of the psyche and will ultimately affect them. Other people smell changes coming twenty or thirty years before they arrive, and the images begin appearing in their dreams and their fantasy life as well as in their artistic creations. I mentioned Yeats before,

with his rather terrifying prophecy of chaos and disorder unleashed in the world. He writes about a "grim beast" whose hour
has come round at last, "slouching toward Bethlehem to be born."
Yeats died just as Hitler was preparing to invade Poland. He wrote
the poem before anyone could have known what was going to
happen in Germany. I would not say it was a "prophecy" of
Hitler, because Yeats was very concerned with astrology and with
the astrological ages, and this was his vision of the Aquarian Age.
But it was also the experience of an overpowering image of imminent chaos and rage bursting from the depths of the collective,
which happened shortly after Yeats' writing, to choose Germany
as one of its midwives.

Millenarian fantasies seem to be cyclical. They seem to erupt
not only every thousand years, but also at the midway points,
perhaps every five hundred years. This is certainly the case with
millenarian movements within the Christian world. And they also
tend to erupt around the periods of great conjunctions. I will
give you an example of how this works. In the Year of Our Lord
1524 as it was called, there was a monumental conjunction of
planets, far more impressive in fact than the ones which are due
in a few years' time because of the number of planets involved.
You can well imagine that in 1524 every astrologer went quite
hysterical, because they only knew of seven heavenly bodies and
all seven were in conjunction in the sign of Pisces. In fact Neptune
was also involved in this conjunction, but they didn't know about
that. Naturally everyone assumed the world was about to end, and
they meant this very literally. No talk of symbols or the collective
unconscious. Pisces is a water sign, and if everything in the heavens
is in Pisces, why, then, the world is obviously going to end by
flood. In the year 1000 everyone also expected the world to end,
and the fact that it hadn't didn't reassure people in 1524. One
astrologer in England built himself an ark, which was rather sensi-
ble in terms of all that water. Obviously people in the sixteenth
century couldn't think in terms of psychological or inner change.
We don't even really understand these things now.

1524 came and went, and not a lot happened. At least, not a
lot happened on a literal level. There were a few wars, but that
was usual, and there was nothing exceptional about France invading Italy or the Austro-Hungarian Empire invading France. There
was a little outbreak of the Black Plague, localised in the south of
France, but it was nothing like the big outbreak in the fourteenth

century which killed a third of the world's population. Over the decade building up to and following the great conjunction in Pisces—and we should remember that these conjunctions have a build-up and a dissemination time just like any other transit or progression—not a lot happened to justify all that terror. The only odd thing was that a very recalcitrant and bad-tempered monk called Martin Luther went around nailing nasty statements about the Church to cathedral doors, and a few people listened.

So the world ended, in the sense that the prevailing and unquestioned view of the world ended. A great crack appeared in the unshakeable bastion of the One True Faith which had dominated the Western world for fifteen hundred years. It is hard for us to understand now just how monumental an event this was. Until Luther there was simply no spiritual reality except the Catholic Church. The general populace, apart from a few rampant heretics, would never have dared to even question this sole road to salvation. What I hope this story suggests to you, as it does to me, is that the ending of the world may occur on subtler levels than the concrete one.

If it's time for something to end, the level on which the ending manifests may vary. This depends also on what is existent in the world which is going to be affected by the emerging new energies. I think it depends very much on the structures existent within society, how flexible or rigid they might be, and how able they are to accommodate change. It also depends very much on the state or quality of consciousness in the individual in society, because nothing can come into expression except in accordance with the form which carries it.

The conjunction of 1524 brought about a change which had already been prophesied and had been in the cooking pot for a long time. It was already in the wind through Henry VIII, who inaugurated his break with the papacy for personal rather than visionary reasons. It simply took the channels which were open. One of the funnier aspects of it is that the astrologers who were in favour of the Reformation, which meant primarily those living in Germany and Switzerland, immediately went around saying that the great conjunction of 1524 was a herald of Luther, that the stars were on his side, that it favoured him and showed that God wanted the Church to change its corrupt ways. You see how we can make anything political, even the planets. Anyway, my feeling is that a similar imminent change is now in the wind. There is an urgent collective yearning which is being expressed in many different ways. I think the trend toward "inner" exploration, which includes the development of new therapies and meditation and astrology and other related quests, reflects this yearning for some alternative vision of reality. Of course if there is a change imminent, there is also going to be a fear of death, because something must die to allow that change to occur. You can see this once again in the dreams of individuals going through deep changes in the personality. They dream of people dying—mother, father, old selves that are outworn—and they often feel a lot of panic and depression until the new thing has emerged and they understand the necessity of the old thing passing away.

You cannot have change without something dying. Any movement of this kind in the psyche tends to collect images of death around it. Religions have always known this, which is why they have always been attached to myths of dying and resurrected gods. An experience of new birth and redemption must always be preceded by the death of an old attitude. Initiation rites from all cultures portray a symbolic death, which heralds the birth of the "saved" or "redeemed" soul. Many artists experience deep depression before the onset of a new creative burst of energy. So I feel that a good deal of the millenarian fear which is around now, as in the past, has as much to do with the anticipation of change as with an actual expectation of destruction in the literal world.

Now I am not implying that I think the next twenty years are going to be absolutely wonderful, any more than they were after the conjunction of 1524. The immediate repercussions of the Reformation were the outbreak of religious wars throughout Europe, which continued into the next century with the Thirty Years' War and which we still have to face in the problem of Northern Ireland. Luther brought not peace, but a sword. I have no doubt that we will have some nasty shocks in the next two decades, even though God is purportedly an Englishman and therefore civilised. We are human, not angelic, and there is a good deal of poverty, oppression and rage throughout the world. The line-up of Uranus, Saturn and Neptune to which we look forward later in this decade is, I am sure, going to produce some upsetting effects politically and economically. You can imagine that it would upset an individual on whose chart it landed, and it will land on the charts of several countries, including Britain, America and the Soviet Union. No doubt it will upset the collective where-ever there are flash points. But that is not quite the same thing as the world ending.

There is a very important difference between the approaching conjunction and the previous occurrences of these planets lining up together. In the earlier centuries when great conjunctions occurred, there was no sense of "individual." No one walked around contemplating the meaning of his identity and his inner self, except for a few Neoplatonists who tended to consider such things important. If a person has a sense of individuality above and beyond the place in society that he occupies, then the effect of collective changes on that person is going to be quite different.

This ties up with something that Jung was preoccupied with. He makes the statement that if there is something wrong with society, then there is something wrong with the individual, and if there is something wrong with the individual then there is something wrong with me. He seems to suggest that when something is due to erupt in the collective, the only safety and sanity to be found is in the firm sense of your own individuality. Otherwise there is no way in which the eruption can be channelled without you becoming a victim of the collective. Then you are blindly carried along with it, and because it is blind and undirected by consciousness it doesn't reason politely and set up careful standards to assess who should pay and who shouldn't. These eruptions run like a torrent, with a ruthlessness that one finds only in blind nature but not in the reflective mind of an individual. One finds it in the natural side of civilised man, the collective instinctual side of him of which he is largely unaware. The collective doesn't theorise. It flows toward its goal in the same way that a baby is born. If you're caught by it, then you must go along with it, and there is no guarantee of the outcome. You might have a Renaissance, which happened around 1500, or you might have a Nazi Germany. Both potentials exist in us, both in society and in individuals. So understandably Jung is concerned with these things, and whenever he writes about the phenomenon of Nazi Germany he repeats again and again his feeling that if we do not want a repetition of this experience, we cannot expect laws and legal structures and religious ideals and political parties to prevent it. We have no hope at all except to see where the battle is being fought within ourselves, and to try to distinguish between our own individual values and the urgent movement that is erupting around us.

I would like to put a diagram up on the blackboard now which I hope will illustrate this rather difficult idea of collective and individual. It comes from Iolande Jacobi's book on Jung's psychology, and I think it is very useful.

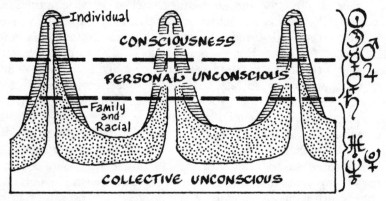

Illustration 1: The structure of the psyche & its relation to the inner and outer planets.

Seen from above, the individual mountain peaks look like completely separate entities. You could say that the top section of each mountain represents the individual personality. On this level we are separate, because we are completely different from each other. Every person has a different horoscope, and when we consider the individual points in a horoscope, such as the ascendant and the midheaven and the sun and moon, we are looking at a map of a distinct individual. In a sense you might say that astrologically, the sun, the moon, Mercury, Venus, Mars, Jupiter and the four angles of the chart concern those energies and needs and characteristics that belong to the individual. Likewise I think the sign and house placements of these planets, and their aspects, describe the individual personality.

Underneath that layer is another layer. The mountains are still separate, but this deeper stratum represents a layer of the psyche which depth psychology has been probing and exploring for some time. Jung called this layer the personal unconscious, and Freud called it the subconscious. This is that side of the personality which lies in shadow, which we cannot see because it's behind us. It's still individual, but most of the time we would prefer not to know that it belongs to us. Here is all the material from childhood,

parental complexes, repressed traumas and wounds, buried emotions, unlived potentials, undeveloped talents. What lies at the top
of the mountain I know to be mine. What lies here in this middle
section belongs to me, but I may be very unaware of it. There's a
threshold between the two areas, and it's the crossing of this
threshold and the freeing of contents trapped in the middle which
occupy many psychotherapeutic efforts. The more a person can
accommodate what is hidden in this shadow-realm, the more
complete he becomes, and the more of his own life he lives.

I think that in astrological terms I would place Saturn on this
threshold between the light and the dark sides of the personality.
Saturn is the ring-pass-not. He rules the boundaries. I think he also
rules the boundary to the lower region here, the place where the
individual mountains meet in one great land mass. These apparently separate forms really emerge from the same roots. They
aren't individual at all, when you view them from this level. And
here I would place the outer planets—Uranus, Neptune and Pluto.
I suppose if any of you are experimenting with Chiron, then he
also would be placed here in the collective realm.

When you look at a horoscope, the inner planets can tell you
a good deal about individual temperament and potential. The
outer planets will tell you much more about the mass to which
the individual belongs. The outer planets have much longer cycles.
Uranus has an eighty-four-year cycle. He spends about seven years
in each sign. Neptune takes about one hundred and sixty-eight
years to go around the zodiac, and spends about fourteen years in
each sign. Pluto takes two hundred and forty-eight years, and his
orbit is elliptical, so he rushes through Scorpio in about eighteen
years and crawls through Taurus in around thirty. These slow
planets have a lot to do with the generation to which a person
belongs. They are concerned with currents within those generation groups. A generation is a very loose entity. We use the word
colloquially when we talk about generation gaps between older
and younger people. But there isn't any rigid line of demarcation
between one generation and the next. The different groups overlap, depending on whether you want to consider Uranus, Neptune
or Pluto. The age difference between an individual and his parents
can vary enormously, because there are women who bear children
at fifteen and men who father children at seventy. There is no
clear biological demarcation for what constitutes a generation. But
there is a clear line of basic attitudes which stamp a seven-year

group who all have Uranus in a certain sign, and a fourteen-year group who all have Neptune in a certain sign, and an eighteen-to-thirty-year group who all have Pluto in a certain sign. So you have a collective of people who all respond to a particular myth or pattern embodied by the outer planet.

A simplistic but reasonable metaphor for this is that of a musical score. There is one underlying rhythm, the rhythm of the bass notes or the drum which defines the entire structure of the piece. Then there is a slightly faster line which adds different qualities and expressions. Finally, there is a melody line on top which dances in and out of the other two, but synchronises with them. So there are several different patterns going on, but together they make a complete piece. For example, if you were born in 1946 you will have Neptune in Libra, and Uranus in Gemini, and Pluto in Leo. If you were born in 1951, Neptune will still be in Libra and Pluto will still be in Leo, but Uranus will have moved into Cancer. So in some respects there are similarities which you will share with everyone who has Neptune in Libra and Pluto in Leo, but you will be different in terms of the expression of Uranus.

One way of seeing the patterns these outer planets make is to consider that different generation groups have a different vision of life. There are certain values which are important to a particular group which might not mean anything at all to the group preceding them and the group following them. I would like to spend some time talking about what each of these outer planets might mean, because I think having some sense of what they represent can help us to understand not only what collective values we carry ourselves, but also how all the different groups weave together to make a pattern within the collective organism. I am convinced that the main effect of the outer planets is through the unconscious. They are not energies which the ego can harness and manipulate and control. They simply don't operate like that. You can always try controlling a transit of Uranus, Neptune or Pluto, but I wish you luck.

Audience: One thing about that map I haven't properly understood is the extent to which people live unconsciously. When you talk about the collective unconscious, do you mean that everybody has the same unconscious? To what extent are people linked to the unconscious? Does the collective unconscious link everybody in this room, for example, at a certain level?

Liz: I can't really give you absolute answers to those questions, anymore than I can illustrate these things properly with a two-dimensional map on a blackboard. I can only talk from what I have seen and experienced, as well as quoting from people like Jung who obviously have seen and experienced considerably more than I have. But yes, there is a very basic level in which all human beings share the same instinctual patterns of behaviour. This not only applies to biological patterns such as sex and aggression and hunger, but to aspirations and religious visions as well. We all seem to have the same psychic structure, and that structure expresses itself in similar myths throughout the ages. Freud spent a lot of time exploring the instinctual patterns of the collective unconscious, although he called it the *id* and not the collective unconscious. He postulated two basic instincts which existed in every human being—the instinct to reproduce and the instinct to destroy. He called these Eros and Thanatos, sexual desire and death-wish. Jung spent a lot of time exploring other drives which he felt were also inherent in every human being. He was very concerned with the religious instinct, the thing in us which takes biological urges and transmutes them into images and symbols which become significant in a religious way. Jung felt that the urge to transmute basic instinctual stuff into transcendent images was as innate a thing as the sexual drive. From what I have seen in my short years of experience, both seem to me to be right. These are drives which are unanimous among everyone. No one is exempt. The manner and quantity of different instincts may vary from one person to another, but no one is without them.

Those are perhaps the most basic levels where we are all the same, where we share the same unconscious urges and patterns. Then there are levels where one group differs slightly from another in the expression of these things. This is apparent from racial and national collectives. If you study the myths from one culture, they may have the same ultimate structure, but the flesh on the bones is different from the myths of another culture. This isn't because of the climate or what they have been taught in school. Myths emerge spontaneously and shape a culture. It seems that after the most basic level of shared human instincts, some differences begin to appear between different peoples. You can see this immediately from a study of comparative religion across cultures. The worship of the Great Mother, for example, was widespread throughout the Mediterranean. You never find her worshipped among northern peoples such as the Teutonic tribes, who are

more addicted to a great Sky-father. This suggests some difference
in the psychic orientation of these different peoples. You can find
rational explanations for this: the Mediterranean cultures were
predominantly agricultural and therefore symbolised the fertility
of the earth as a divine Great Woman, while the northern tribes
tended to be nomads and herdsmen who were used to wide
spaces, where weather and winds and harsh sun and other phenomena from heaven were more important. I would not want
to get into an argument about whether the external world shapes
the archetypal image or the archetypal image shapes the external
world. In the end you must simply consider these different gods,
which embody the values of a people. We all share a common
Judeo-Christian heritage. Whether you are a practising Christian
or Jew makes very little difference. This level is unconscious, and
its energy is vital and alive whether your ego agrees with those
viewpoints or not.

Our Judeo-Christian heritage is embedded in our blood and
bones, regardless of whether we are technically religious. The
image of God throughout Judeo-Christian culture is the same,
despite the ideological differences of Catholic, Anglican, Mormon,
Hassidic Jew, Reform Jew or whatever. We worship one god and
we call that god HE. God is male, God is spirit, God is eternal and
omniscient, and God is not matter. We have many different sub-
cultures represented here in this room. Some of you may be
Celtic, some Saxon, some Jewish, some German. Each of you will
have a more individual mythology that belongs to your racial
background. These things are like geological strata that make
many different layers and designs, beneath which the same bedrock lies.

I don't think racial and national myths appear in the birth
chart, anymore than the sex of a person is represented. These
are the unknown factors which are not described by the person's
horoscope, which I hope you will have all realised. There is a mysterious centre of the personality which is also not in the horoscope. I am sure you will understand what this means if you
consider that the chart in front of you could be the chart of a
chicken. It might be that of an opera house. There is nothing
in that horoscope that announces that it's the natal chart of a
human being. And there is nothing in the horoscope that tells you
whether it's a German or an Italian or a Swede or a Lebanese Jew
or a Chinese. These are mysterious factors that you must consider

in conjunction with the horoscope. They will affect the ways in which the person expresses his horoscope, just as the fact of whether the person's a man or a woman will affect the expression of the chart. The person who comes from a background full of Indian or Chinese myths is going to build his individuality on bedrock which is different from the person who is drawing from a Teutonic or Anglo-Saxon background. An Arab may have the same horoscope as an Englishman but his religious symbols and cultural values make him use the horoscope differently. This isn't because of teaching or conscious values. It's innate, it's a psychological inheritance as powerful as genetic inheritance. This is the strange thing about it. You can take a person who has been transplanted very early in life and educated in the ideas and laws and attitudes of an entirely different culture, but in the dreams the symbols of the ancient roots immediately surface.

Jung was convinced that we cannot outgrow or escape our roots without suffering some psychological damage. That doesn't mean that the individual can't develop himself above and beyond what his culture has to offer. But somehow we must learn to cope with the collective from which we spring, because it is as important a part of psychic life as the more personal qualities we believe to be our own.

The outer planets don't describe those basic mythic images like the Great Mother or Wotan or whatever. I think they describe a different aspect of the collective, an aspect which is constantly moving and changing. There are great movements of ideas and visions which erupt in society and find their way into the mouths of many people all at once. The outer planets don't describe racial or national myths, because everyone in the world has the same outer planets in the horoscope, and an American and a Japanese both born in 1944 will both have Uranus in Gemini and Neptune in Libra despite their different gods. Now I would like to consider these planets in more detail, because I don't think we understand them very well. I certainly don't understand them very well, and most textbook descriptions understand them even less. As usual I have found more help from reading mythology and other symbolic languages than from orthodox astrological texts. If you pick up one of the older, classic astrology texts, it is likely to tell you that Uranus means change, inventiveness, revolution and perversity. Neptune means drugs, deception, confusion. Pluto means death and rebirth. Those words sound very profound and meaningful. They're useful sometimes, such as trying to tell a client under a Neptune transit that he's likely to feel confused. But what do these planets really mean?

Uranus is the first god in Greek myth, the heavenly father who engenders the universe. He emerges from the womb of Gaia, who is Mother or Chaos, and then he mates with her. Uranus belongs to the air, to the sky. He is a sky-god. He is a god of ideas, and flies on the wings of thought. In esoteric circles this is sometimes called the Divine Mind. Plato wrote about the Divine Ideas, upon which all worldly forms are patterned. It's as though something exists before the universe is formed, which is the *idea* of a universe. So Uranus has something to do with a pattern, an ordering force which does not yet have body. Uranus comes to a bad end in myth, because he's castrated by his son Kronos. His severed genitals fall into the ocean, which is fertilised by his seed, and out of the foam springs Aphrodite, the goddess of love. Uranus is a fertility-god, but not in an earthy sense. He fertilises with creative thought, with spirit. I think we can see his footsteps in history whenever a great new creative idea erupts in the collective. Around the time of the discovery of Uranus, the idea of democracy and the freedom of the individual was a powerful force that changed society. During the French Revolution, the justification of the Reign of Terror was the cry of liberty, equality, fraternity. The French monarchy was deposed in the name of an idea, and the idea was a tremendous force which generated great changes in France. Ideas can be moving forces in the world, just as powerful as economic pressures. They erupt from the collective and seize the minds of a people, and then there is nothing that can be done to stop it, even attempts at suppression.

During the Italian Renaissance another idea took hold of people which caused enormous changes in society. This was the idea that man's nature was divine. That may sound terribly simple, but it wasn't simple then. It was heresy. If man is God, then he doesn't need intermediaries to interpret God's will to him. He's capable of experiencing his own contact with the divine. If he doesn't need intermediaries, then he doesn't need the Church for his salvation. He might need it as a fellowship or an inspiration, but he isn't dependent upon it for his experience of grace. That idea contained immense power. It allowed men to explore other philosophies and gods without fear of being tainted. It spawned the creative flowering which we call the Renaissance. It restored dignity to man, who was no longer a mere worm stained by original sin who had to live his life consumed by guilt and fear. Pico della Mirandola's oration to man begins: "What a great miracle is man! He partakes of the nature of both gods and daimons."

This kind of eruption of a powerful idea which seizes men's imaginations is what I associate with Uranus. The trouble with these ideas is that they come from the heavenly world, and so they are usually a little too advanced for the world at the time. The divine dignity of man which captured the creative minds of the Renaissance was a little too much to swallow, and so it was duly suppressed because Uranian ideas are inevitably too far ahead of the culture which breeds them. If an idea suddenly bursts into being in the outer world, it has had to travel up from the depths, and it's coloured by the sign through which Uranus is passing. That sign represents the sphere of life which will be changed or transformed by the new idea. A few people become its mouthpieces, and it starts to work like yeast within society. But it will take a very long time before the forms of the world can be altered enough to accommodate it. Or you might say that it will take a very long time before individual people are capable of integrating it into their lives without some frightening distortions. Jung thought it took around eighty years for some new content emerging from the collective unconscious to work its way through the different levels of society. He was making an intuitive assessment, since of course there is no way we can measure such things. But this time span he gives is roughly the time it takes Uranus to return to any given sign. Uranus' cycle, as I said, is eighty-four years.

It's the prophets and visionaries and artists who seem to catch the new idea while it's still boiling and bubbling in the depths. Eventually it becomes something popular among the mass of people, but usually by that time they've burned the prophet at the stake or ruined him. Then they say, "We have a wonderful new idea. Why don't we make a set of laws which incorporate it?" Then they give honour to the handful of Uranian people who first had the idea, even though it was originally heretical. The problem of Uranus in myth is that Saturn-Kronos castrates him. It's only much later that he's regenerated as Aphrodite and translated into something creative and harmonious which the world likes.

We can go back to our map of the mountains and imagine a Uranian idea travelling slowly upward from the bedrock into the

lives and minds of individual people. If you remember, I placed
Saturn on the borders between the individual and the collective.
So Saturn is the first thing that the new idea hits on its way
upward and outward into the world. Saturn is the boundary which
separates me from you. So the people who will feel the rush upward of these new movements and ideas are, I think, the people
who have Saturn and Uranus in strong aspect in the birth chart. I
think this group of people, particularly those who have Saturn
conjuncting Uranus, get the itch first. They sense the need for
change on an ideological level, and they become the willing or
unwilling mouthpieces for the new idea before it becomes something acceptable in society.

A person who has Uranus in strong aspect to the sun or the
moon or Mercury or Mars will also feel this rush of anticipation
about the new idea, but it will affect that person differently. It
will express itself through some personal area of life. If Uranus
aspects Venus, for example, then the person will act out that new
idea through his relationships, without necessarily being aware of
it as a "new idea." But the impact is very different when Uranus
hits Saturn. There is a jarring with that contact. I think it creates
an urgency. Something is knocking on the door very loudly and
persistently, and if you don't listen then it threatens to break the
door down. And Saturn, because he's the form-builder and is
concerned with worldly issues, feels the necessity to do something
practical with the new idea. The moon and Uranus may simply
feel very rebellious, and Mercury and Uranus may devote a lot of
time to studying and thinking about the new thing. But Saturn
must build it into his world.

Neptune is very different from his heavenly, airy brother.
Neptune is a god of water in myth, and governs the depths of the
sea. He rules a realm where everything is ambiguous. Forms blend
and dissolve, and colours merge. Water is one of the primary
symbols of the world of feeling. It's also one of the most ancient
images for the feminine womb out of which life emerges. The
name Mary has its roots in the word *mer*, which is the sea. This is
the sea which is the womb of life. It's the world of the emotions
and the imagination.

When Uranus captures a person, it's through an idea which
takes possession of him. When Neptune captures a person, it's
through the world of dreams and longings and yearnings. Neptune
often manifests through what we experience as glamourous or

fashionable. The way in which glamour affects us is very different from the impact of an idea or an ideology. Of course they can join together. Socialism can be both a logical ideology and also a glamourous fashion. But the feeling of magic and glamour is a separate thing from the feeling of truth which accompanies a powerful idea. When a style of clothing abruptly becomes fashionable, all of a sudden everyone is wearing it and no one really knows why. The style appears in every shop window and every fashion magazine and even people who like to think of themselves as highly individual turn up in it. Several designers may turn up with the same thing at the same time and they haven't stolen the design from each other, it's more that some image or "look" is surfacing and the more intuitive or creative person gives shape to it. Suddenly everyone has long hair, or suddenly skirt lengths go up or down. Suits from the 1940's become *de rigeur*. Stiletto heels are back in style. Science fiction films flood the cinema. Punk is the latest craze.

These are Neptunian trends. They creep up on us from a feeling level. They're not ideologies. They may at first strike you as ridiculous or banal, because they seem to have so little to do with our lonely strivings toward growth and consciousness. But these trends are tremendously powerful. They are responsible for vast sums of money moving back and forth within society, and they touch us on very subtle levels. I think they are more important than they seem, because they reflect yearnings and dreams and longings that are translated into images which the consumer eagerly buys. It's as if all the deep longings in the collective manifest themselves in this way, whether it's a religious movement or a fashion trend. This is where we are reaching blindly toward something divine, which embodies itself in the length of a skirt.

I have been very struck by Warren Kenton's books on the Kabbalah, where he connects Neptune with the very top of the Tree of Life. This highest point on the Tree is the ineffable, the glimpse of the divine which is the most human beings can comprehend of the mystery of the godhead. It's called the Crown, and it's the place where the sense of lonely separateness is dissolved into an experience of unity and bliss. When we are compelled by fashions, we are experiencing something that surfaces from the deepest yearnings of the heart, and I don't think that clothing and cosmetics and visions of what is beautiful are any less valid carriers of this than religious symbols. These things emerge from a level that is not concerned with our ethics of right and wrong. They make us feel better, they take us out of ourselves.

Neptune is also connected with the figure of the mermaid or melusine in fairy tales, who beckons the mortal man to submerge himself in the magic depths of the lake or sea. In rites of baptism, these waters cleanse and purify. They can also disintegrate the personality. They are terribly enticing, because you no longer have to strive and struggle and experience separation and conflict and loss. In the depths of the sea you merge with the source. Religion might call that a union with God, while more reductive psychologies might call it a longing to return to the maternal womb.

So the apparently banal trends of fashion tell us a lot about what an entire collective yearns for. These trends are symbols. If you look at what is fashionable in this way, it's quite fascinating. It's a pictorial story of what the collective secretly needs and longs for, although these longings could never be translated into worldly terms that made any sense. The god who lives in the depths of the ocean spins out a dream. Neptune passes through a particular sign and suddenly the collective reaches toward that sign and its symbols because that is where the soul beckons. When Neptune moves on into the next sign then the symbols go dry, and what was fashionable for fourteen years now seems ridiculous. So we all rush out and buy the new style.

Now perhaps we can consider some of the possible meanings of Pluto. There are many curious features about this planet which make it a kind of renegade. He doesn't obey the rules. His orbit is elliptical, and there is a phase in the orbit where he is actually closer to the earth than Neptune, although the plane of the orbit is slanted slightly and isn't aligned with the plane of the other planets' orbits. This phase of Pluto's orbit seems to occur when he is transiting through Scorpio. Pluto will be entering Scorpio in November 1983 for around eighteen years, and of course this phase of his orbit is the passage through his own sign.

Dane Rudhyar attaches considerable significance to the period when Pluto is closer to the earth than Neptune, and talks about it as a "fertilising." I decided to investigate some of the historical movements that occurred during the various times when Pluto moved through Scorpio, and unearthed some rather interesting things. For example, Pluto went into Scorpio in the last decade of the fifteenth century. That time is extremely important because it marked the dawn of the Florentine Renaissance. On a cultural level it was certainly a period of immense fertilisation, a true rebirth of lost knowledge and spiritual vision. The actual incidents which led to this massive explosion of human creativity are typically Plutonian. Cosimo de Medici, the ruler of Florence, had a taste for collecting lost Greek manuscripts, and some of these fell into his hands after the sack of Constantinople in 1453. One of these was a strange document which was later called the *Corpus Hermeticum*. It was actually written in the second century A.D., but Cosimo's translator, Marsilio Ficino, thought he had found a text more ancient even than the Bible, and spread around the idea that a great and ancient sage called Hermes Trismegistus had written the text. The philosophy embedded in this text altered the thinking of the whole of Europe.

The *Corpus Hermeticum* was not Christian, and it led to a flowering of interest in the pagan gods as well as a fascination for the Kabbalah, the Tarot, and talismanic magic. It postulated that the universe was one great unified life, and that what was above was a reflection of what was below. It spoke about the reincarnation of the soul. It praised the dignity and divinity of man, the great miracle who is both beast and god. This world-view we would now call Hermetic, or Neoplatonic. At the time it was an immense heresy, because of its overriding injunction that the gods were found in life, in flesh and in form, as much as in heaven.

A number of very important people were born under this transit of Pluto in Scorpio, as well as the main philosophical thrust of the Renaissance. Among these people was Martin Luther, whose impact on the religion of the time was monumental. Another was Paracelsus, who is sometimes considered the father of modern medicine. These people born with Pluto in Scorpio anchored the ideas which the transit brought by their life-work. They transformed some of the apparently unchanging structures of society. Any Renaissance always implies the death of something, and the age of the Church Fathers and the narrowness of medieval thought came to an end when Pluto entered Scorpio at the end of the fifteenth century. I suppose it would be forgivable to say that this transit ended the era of medieval man.

There was another transit of Pluto through Scorpio in 1240. This period is another time when strange philosophical ideas began to percolate through the Christian world. It was the time of the Knights Templar and of the flowering of Kabbalism in

Spain. It was also the time of the troubadours and the Courts of Love. This period is sometimes called the High Medieval Renaissance, and it contains the same peculiar flowering of arcane ideas that the later Renaissance does. Alchemy was also at its height at this time, and the philosophy of Ramon Lull, which was once again Kabbalistic and Neoplatonic, was spreading around Europe. I can of course be accused of reading things into these two periods because I am looking for something, but any student of Hermetic philosophy quickly discovers that it has a cyclical life. It erupts into the collective for a brief time, and then its adherents are persecuted and it goes underground, only to erupt again around two hundred and fifty years later. That is of course a cycle of Pluto. Therefore it didn't surprise me to discover later that the transit of Pluto through Scorpio during the eighteenth century, around 1740 to be precise, coincided with the rise of Freemasonry and with the birth of Franz Mesmer, who incorporated the Hermetic world-view into a scientific method of exploring the human psyche which eventually fathered modern psychology.

I am becoming convinced that Pluto is concerned with a certain vision of the universe, which is basically Hermetic and which has a tendency to surface when the supporting structures of society begin to break apart. Man has always explained his reality in physical terms, and has built his social structures in an extroverted way. Something seems to happen when Pluto enters his own sign that concerns cracks in the wall of this extroverted world-view. It is as though there is something which we loosely call "lost knowledge," which is really knowledge of the universe that comes from a different place than the senses and their perceptions. This "lost knowledge" suddenly surfaces, wearing a new costume, when Pluto moves into his own sign.

The fact that Pluto is soon to move into Scorpio once again has of course raised many questions in my mind. If I have really found some kind of pattern in Pluto's transits through history, then the ancient Hermetic world-view ought to be on the horizon now, just getting ready to make itself felt again. Of course I can see its tracks in Jung's psychology, which is, in the end, built upon the same world-view after you grapple with terms like "collective unconscious" and "synchronicity" and "archetype." Jung's psychological vision of life, which he tried to anchor firmly in observation and empiric research, is in the end cut of the same cloth as the *Corpus Hermeticum.* I am also inclined to look at the recent flowering of astrology and its allies, the Tarot and the *I Ching*, as another sign of the same thing. Astrology also seems to have a cyclical flowering, and not surprisingly it trots alongside Hermetic philosophy, because it's one of the best vehicles for the vision of what is above being like what is below.

I don't think that this is really philosophy in the sense that Uranus is tied to conceptual visions of the universe. This is some kind of profound sensing of the nature of life itself, which has been articulated in some very funny language each time Pluto goes through Scorpio. It's as though this profound sensing cuts through all the religious dogmas and political visions and penetrates to the very core of man's soul. It's also a perennial philosophy, or world-view, and it has been hacked to pieces over and over again only to rise once more in new clothing. These movements which I am calling Plutonian seem to attract a good deal of anger and persecution from collective authority, but they are indestructible. They keep coming back again and again. There is a common root behind Freemasonry and Lullism and Neoplatonism and Hermetism and depth psychology, although I'm sure a lot of people would get very angry hearing me make those connections.

Pluto is the great time-keeper of the collective. All these little individual mountain peaks have gone their way for a while happily thinking they've solved all the questions and mysteries of life, and they've built a society according to one model or another and now they know all about the nature of God and man. Then along comes Pluto and something is revealed which holds incredible depths and blows apart that very complacent set of values. Pluto heralds the death of religions and cosmologies, and offers the same intense vision to replace them each time.

I'm sure you will have worked out by now that the individuals who are going to be most sensitive to these things are those who have Saturn and Pluto in strong aspect in the birth chart, just as Saturn-Uranus people hear the voice of the new idea and Saturn-Neptune people smell the scent of the new mystical vision. I see that some of you are laughing at this as though it makes sense to you. I think Saturn-Pluto conjunctions glimpse the approaching death of society's gods and the gradual re-emergence of that ancient vision of life. I suspect that some Saturn-Pluto people help that death along by playing the role of saboteur, while others immerse themselves in the perennial philosophy. But these people are buffeted most strongly, because they must embody Pluto in some way in their lives.

Audience: How did these planets come to be named?

Liz: That's a very curious thing. The man who discovered Uranus called it after himself, and for a while the planet was known as Herschel. That's really an offense against aesthetic taste. After Saturn, Jupiter, Venus, Mars and Mercury comes Herschel. I don't know why it eventually got called Uranus, but somehow the name and the meaning of the planet are synchronous. There is also a curious synchronicity between the time when the planet is discovered and the emergence in society of values and experiences which the planet represents symbolically. It's as though the planet breaks upon consciousness in both a literal and a symbolic way. I can't really answer you as to why Uranus is called Uranus and Neptune, Neptune. I can only say that in some mysterious fashion they get the right names.

Audience: What about Pluto?

Liz: Well, the story is that it was named for Mickey Mouse's dog, because Percival Lowell, who discovered the planet, had a daughter who was very attached to this dog called Pluto. I think it's an apocryphal story, but it's as good as any other. Probably Pluto was called Pluto because it's so far out in the dark depths of space. Since all the other planets bear mythological names, Pluto would be the obvious name for a planet so hidden and mysterious. We project our mythic fantasies onto the cosmos. The same thing could be argued about the seven planets known to ancient astronomers. Mercury is called Mercury because he's the fastest and tiniest of the planets. Mars is red and therefore called Mars because that's the god of war and bloodshed. I think there is justification for suggesting that we project our images onto physical planets because they carry physical features which connect with the fantasies. But that doesn't explain why the solar system should so agreeably provide a hook for those projections. Pluto might have been named because someone thought the ancient god of the underworld would be a fitting figure for a planet hidden in the underworld of space. But Pluto also behaves like the god of the underworld, and for that I can offer no answer. The name is synchronous with the meaning. Probably there is some deep law at work, but I could not possibly offer a rational explanation to a scientist.

The values and visions which belong to Uranus, Neptune and Pluto were of course around long before the planets were discovered. They have always been with us. There are people in history who have embodied these values and visions, like Paracelsus who had the sun conjunct Pluto in Scorpio. I don't think there is any difference between a modern individual with strong outer planet contacts who is in touch with the movements in the collective, and a twelfth century individual who has these same contacts and who is also their mouthpiece. But there was no collective conception of what these planets might mean before the time of their discovery. They couldn't be anchored in external life. They were probably discovered when their time was ripe. I'm inclined to revert to a more archaic way of looking at things, and tend to see the planets as something alive and numinous. They were once called gods, and if you prefer the term archetype it doesn't lessen their mysterious power in any way. I don't see why we shouldn't see the planets as evolving and changing in the same way that other life forms evolve and change. Perhaps when it's time for them to be embodied in the world, they're discovered by somebody's telescope. That, at any rate, is my fantasy about it.

Audience: Does that mean that things may happen in the collective unconscious which can't be lived out in the world?

Liz: I suppose you could say that. I think things happen in an individual's dreams which can't be lived out in his life often for many years, if ever. If a child of five dreams of meeting a magical androgynous figure with bird-claws and wings who can make gold out of mud, he isn't going to be able to do very much except tell somebody he had a very strange dream. That may represent a potential which he gets a glimpse of when he's seventy and has flogged many long miles. I'm sure the same applies for the collective. One individual who glimpses a potential vision for society may be very fired by it during his lifetime, but everyone just laughs at him because it will take another five hundred years before the collective can do anything with it. The eruption or the change may affect an individual, but it can't yet affect society because society isn't ready for it, so it goes underground for another cycle.

This has always been the role of the prophet and the artist. The prophet can sense these potentials. He can read the dreams of the collective which are sent by the gods, and he paints the painting which is really the voice of the collective reaching out for its dreams. I mentioned Yeats earlier, and there are countless others, individual voices who sense the future unfolding. But usually these people don't make much impact during their time. They are seen as curiosities, and it's generally long after they're dead that anyone recognises the truth of their vision. If you have come into personal contact with such people then you may be profoundly affected, and your life may be changed. But society as a whole may suddenly start giving the person's work value , after two hundred years, claiming that this was a great poet. They recognise it only after the poet's vision has already surfaced and become something recognisable by the mass of people.

Lecture Two

This morning I would like to begin by discussing a few examples of the workings of outer planet conjunctions with Saturn, which I began to touch on last night. This will be specific interpretive material, and I am going to focus on the conjunctions that have occurred during this century between Saturn and Uranus, Saturn and Neptune, and Saturn and Pluto. I have been accumulating a rather strange body of information on the Saturn-Pluto conjunction from clients who were born between 1946 and 1948, when it was in Leo. Before I begin with this material, do any of you have any burning questions or thoughts that have come out of last night's session?

Audience: How about giving your own chart?

Liz: I never give my own chart. Are there any other burning questions?

Audience: Can you say something about Pluto in Libra?

Liz: I can try. Let's begin with what Pluto means. Pluto destroys or breaks down or heralds the end of certain kinds of forms, and reveals a more eternal or more profound vision beneath. If you consider those spheres of life which Libra rules—which means predominantly relationships, not only marriage and the concept of marriage but also world relationships, diplomacy between countries, political treaties and arrangements like NATO, alliances between political parties and so on—then you can get some idea of where Pluto is going to overturn old methods and attitudes. One of the effects of the transit of Pluto through Libra is certainly the altering of existing attitudes toward relationship. I think it is certainly connected with the rise of the feminist movement. Of course these issues have always been with us, and individuals have always struggled with them, but they have never assumed the proportions of a movement. Divorce laws are changing, contracts between people who are cohabiting but are not married are assuming new importance, homosexual relationships are gradually becoming more recognised.

I also think that our concepts of alignment between nations are also changing radically during this transit. There has been a certain amount of *naïveté* about which countries are "good guys" and which are "bad guys," and about who has the right to interfere with whose development. My generation was certainly brought up with very defined black-and-white ideas about good nations with a good way of life and evil nations who are the enemy. Pluto is still in Libra and will be there for another two or three years, and I am hesitant to make any concrete predictions about what it will do. There is a conjunction of Saturn and Pluto in 1982 and 1983, and this is liable to crystallise whatever changes are going to happen. Wars usually break out under Saturn-Pluto conjunctions or just preceding them, and that may radically affect who is whose friend in the international alignments. When Saturn conjuncts one of the outer planets, things have a way of manifesting in the world in a very literal fashion, which is not so obvious when the outer planet is passing alone through a sign. Something happens on the world stage when Saturn is around, so I would rather not attempt to foresee more than some kind of crisis and realignment of allegiances nationally and politically. I think the changes in marriage and divorce laws and in attitudes toward relationships are increasingly obvious. Pluto entered Libra for the first time in October 1971, and we have come a long way since then in terms of greater sophistication and insight into the dilemmas of partnership. Things will never be the same again. Although individuals have always tried to make headway in these spheres, the collective has been stuck in some very rigid patterns which are now beginning to break up and reform.

I'm going to put this diagram of the mountains back on the blackboard. I would like you to keep the diagram in mind, because I think it helps to ground this paradox of collective and individual. Several people have asked me to talk about Chiron, and I am rather ambivalent about doing that, firstly because I don't know very much about him. Secondly, I am not sure how seriously Chiron will be treated by astrologers in the future. There was a great flurry of interest around the time the "miniplanet" was discovered between Saturn and Uranus, but in the end it may turn out a bit like the asteroids—a sort of specialised refinement rather than a main component of the horoscope. Anyway I think I will do what I can with Chiron now and get him out of the way before I move on to individual horoscopes.

The first article on Chiron appeared before any real research had been gathered, and it had a kind of irresistible intellectual attractiveness. Because the planet or asteroid or whatever it is wandered into the solar system rather later than the other planets, Chiron is a maverick, a newcomer. The authors of the article connected this maverick quality with the Sagittarian Centaur, who apparently wanders about shooting arrows off into space and chasing various things. Centaurs don't, in fact, behave like this. The two main mythic figures, Chiron and Nessus, are quite the opposite. But the kind of intuitive logic that made the authors of the Chiron article assign it as the ruler of Sagittarius is terribly attractive. The deduction was that since Chiron is a wanderer and a maverick among planets, therefore it should co-rule Sagittarius and should mean things like the wanderlust and desire for change and expansion in a person's horoscope.

I am not very happy about that interpretation. It came too quickly and without any real empiric backup. I think we must start experimenting with Chiron in our own charts and see what he does. I have done a little work with Chiron in clients' charts, but I am still very hazy about the meaning. I have a few clues, but no more than that. I've also tried another approach to Chiron, which is the thing I've already mentioned—the strange synchronicity between the time of a new planet's discovery and the emergence of the values the planet represents into collective consciousness. It's worth looking first at the discovery of Uranus, Neptune and Pluto to demonstrate this phenomenon.

Uranus was discovered between the American Revolution and the French Revolution. Both these political events concerned an eruption into society of an idea—the idea of the democratic state governed by and for the people, where society has the right to elect its ruler. Now democracy was an idea that was tossed around in ancient Greece, but it meant something rather different. The Greek idea of democracy included a large slave population, and the people eligible for election had to come from a particular social class with particular training. Greek democracy was certainly never government by and for the people. It was government by a noble élite who elected each other in and out of office. The vision of a democratic state is not new, but no nation had ever been capable of achieving anything near it until those two revolutions in the eighteenth century. I think the very profound idea that an individual should not be bound by inheritance and ties of blood is a truly Uranian idea. It places consciousness and freedom of will above nature. Whether it is practically possible in a complete sense is not the point. The discovery of Uranus coincided with the very first attempt to build a nation's constitution on such ideas.

Uranus also coincided with the dawn of the technological age. I think there is once again an idea behind this kind of movement—the same idea that man should not be bound and limited by nature, but can by the power of his intellect find methods and implements to break the control of the forces of nature. This is the same ethic as the one underlying the political movements of the time. Man should by the power of his mind be allowed to become master of the world that he lives in. When you realise how much men bowed to the idea of fate and the bondage of nature in earlier centuries, then you will see what a very different spirit entered the collective at the time of Uranus' discovery.

Pluto is also very interesting to consider in terms of what was happening in the world at the time of his discovery. Pluto's finding coincides first of all with the rise of the Third Reich. I will be referring again to this connection, because I feel there is a good deal we don't understand about Pluto and I am convinced there is a relationship with the psychological phenomenon of Nazi Germany. What happened in World War Two is still a great mystery. It cannot be explained away by economic and political analyses. Something very archaic and dark erupted into society. We now have a tendency simply to blame Germany, but I am not convinced it's that simple. Something was unleashed around the time of Pluto's discovery which I think has something to do with the collective shadow. Obviously there have been other eruptions of this kind in history. There have been massacres and witch hunts and genocide in every country in the world. But this latest version of it also contained a successful manipulation of those more bestial or archaic forces, and I think the issue of power over these energies is connected with Pluto.

There have always been mad dictators, but I think the Third Reich was a first because it used psychological knowledge to further its ends. Dictators usually dictate with armies, not with the power of hypnosis over the masses. I am sure that the positive features of this kind of insight are very bound up with the development of psychotherapy and analysis, but so far we have really seen primarily the worst of Pluto. Every planet has its dark and its light side. Perhaps the darkness of Pluto has as much to do with his repression as it does with any innate malevolence on the part of the planet. But I feel the kind of power issues that emerged in the 1930's are very relevant to the meaning of Pluto.

I am sure there are many more correlations to be found with the discovery of the outer planets. Neptune, for example, was discovered around the same time that hypnosis began to be used and the first real explorations into the unconscious began. So when I began to consider Chiron, I understandably asked myself what new things might be emerging in the collective which are completely different from what has happened before and which might be synchronous with the finding of a new planet.

The thing which struck me first, which of course may be a good intuition or a merely subjective fantasy, is that the attitude toward the body is changing in an entirely new way. Perhaps the name Chiron is in the end as appropriate as Uranus, Neptune and Pluto are, because in myth Chiron is primarily a healer. He's not just your ordinary garden-variety centaur. He is a full-fledged god, brother to Zeus, and he is a teacher, a sage and a physician or healer. He knows all the secrets of nature—he distills potions and works with herbs and knows alchemy and teaches the wisdom of the earth to men. He's an earth deity, and his particular skill is that of healing the body.

This seems to me to be important because something very interesting is beginning to happen in the field of medicine. Of course "fringe" or alternative medicine has been around for a very long time, but it has mainly been considered fringe. The body and the psyche have not been seen as a single unity since the collapse of the Renaissance, and the belief in that unity was a mystical one rather than one based on empiric evidence. But there seems to be a gradual movement now toward a unified vision of body and psyche, and this is totally new in terms of science and medicine. Psychiatry, which is the poor bastard hybrid in between, has never successfully bridged the chasm, but I am seeing more and more doctors take seriously not only the findings of acupuncture and homeopathy and herbalism, but also the findings of psychology about the inner meaning of physical symptoms.

I think this is also connected with the emerging realisation on the part of physicists that matter has intelligence. There is a vast no-man's land between the material sciences and the study of the psyche, whether it's called psychology or some more esoteric name. So I have been suspecting that if we have truly discovered a new planet, this is the great new uncharted territory we are entering synchronous with Chiron's discovery. I'm not sure how true all this is, but it's a very creative fantasy.

What I have found with individual horoscopes is that Chiron does seem to behave like a full-fledged outer planet. By that I mean that the crises and difficulties in the house in which Chiron is placed are beyond the control of the individual, and the changes which occur under Chiron progressions and transits expand and alter the consciousness of the person undergoing them. Outer planets have a certain feeling which is very different from the inner planets. If you have a difficult aspect to Mars by progression, for example, or a conjunction of Saturn or Jupiter by transit, you may discover things about yourself, but they are things which you can handle, and which belong to the human realm. You may get insights about discipline or self-sufficiency or loneliness or defensiveness under Saturn, but these are issues that can be integrated into your personal life if you have the stamina to deal with them. They may hurt, and you may not like them, but they don't raise the hair at the back of your neck. The progressions and transits of the inner planets concern issues which emerge from the top two levels of the mountain peaks in the diagram. These may be unconscious issues, but it's your unconscious, rather than the collective one. I realise that is a harder distinction than actually occurs in practise, but it gives a rough idea.

With the outer planets, on the other hand, you are introduced to an unknown realm. The outer planets stretch consciousness beyond the individual himself. They confront the person with mysteries, with fate, with forces that are much larger than his own little life. In the pictographic language of China, the word *crisis* is a combination of danger and opportunity. It's dangerous because it involves elements which are alien and unknown to the personality. It's an opportunity because it offers potential for the personality to enlarge and connect with something more transpersonal. The outer planets usually shatter one's entrenched views about the nature of reality.

From the little I have been able to observe, Chiron behaves in this way. Things seem to happen, either inside or outside, where ego control is simply inappropriate. The ego can't get its grubby little hands on these changes and turn them into something personally manageable. Personal will seems to be quite irrelevant with the outer planets. It's much more important for the inner planets, because this concerns owning and giving direction to your own drives and needs. But with the outer planets, pitting your will against them only messes you up badly. The most frequent occurrence I have found so far with Chiron transits and progressions is illness. Usually it's the kind of illness that requires some understanding of its origins and its meaning, rather than simple treatment in an ordinary sense. Illness is one of the prime movers for us, because it awakens so many fears and terrors and fantasies that centre around what the body means.

There are classic crisis situations that are popular with the outer planets. One is that relationships or marriages threaten to break apart. Another is the change in vocation or direction, whether it's voluntary or forced from without. I already mentioned illness. Spiritual or religious crises are common, and so are the deaths of parents. These events are usually what we consider to be the causes for inner change, but events such as these coincident with outer planet movements are reflections, rather than causes. They correspond to some profound internal change which can't be understood or lived until an outer event occurs that completely changes one's life patterns.

There is one other thing about Chiron that I have noticed, which makes me suspect even more that it's earthy in nature rather than Sagittarian. Chiron appears with great regularity in synastry on close relationships. I've found this particularly with sexual relationships. This has again led me to consider Chiron as having something to do with the nature of the body itself. Usually sexuality is considered in traditional astrology to be under the rule of Venus and Mars, and also Pluto if you consider a more psychological view of it. But these planets describe emotional needs and qualities to which we are attracted. They don't really tell us why we should find some physical bodies beautiful and others repulsive. There is a mystery about body chemistry which no amount of psychological mapping seems to be able to answer. Some of the newer therapies such as bioenergetics concern themselves with body energy. We're back again to the borderland between psychic and physical.

This is really all I can say about Chiron. I haven't the foggiest notion how to interpret it in a practical way by house and sign. I said that I have only intimations. I have a very strong feeling that it's earthy in nature, and because of this, if we must assign it to a sign of the zodiac, I would suggest either Taurus or Virgo, both of which share a ruler with another sign. Virgo is not very comfortable with Mercury because there are attributes in Virgo that aren't really described by the Mercurial rulership. And I think there are qualities in Taurus which don't really fit Venus. But you will have to experiment for yourselves, because these are intuitions, not gospel truths.

Audience: Could you say a little more about outer planets bringing crises? Do you mean by transit?

Liz: Yes, I mean when an outer planet makes a strong aspect by transit to something in the birth chart. The thing that is threatened and changed is described by the planet that is aspected. For example, if Uranus is transiting opposite your sun, then you must look at your sense of individuality. The sun describes our basic view of ourselves, our feeling of being special, separate individuals. If Uranus hits this point, it's as though the planet is saying, "Sorry, but this just won't do. Your view of reality is too limited. I'll just hammer you a little bit and make a few cracks in that solid wall, and then you'll discover that life is different from what you imagined and you're also different from what you imagined." Of course people react very differently to such an experience. Some people say, "Good heavens, I've had a major revelation." Others get terribly angry and blame everyone in sight for shaking their lives up. Some people welcome the possibility of change, while others fight it and therefore bring the roof down on their heads because the planet has nowhere else to go except into events.

I think this is a very difficult issue for many people to take. You can meet someone who has been plodding along in the same job for twenty years, with the same attitudes and the same rigidity. He's never allowed any new potentials to develop in his life because he's playing safe. Along comes an outer planet, and suddenly something terrible happens. He unconsciously sets himself up to lose his job, or it's just fate that he loses it. Then he has to start thinking of what his life has really been about all these years. It's very hard and very painful, and if he fights against it then things just go from bad to worse. But if he takes the situation as something needed, something which can help him grow and develop, then he's greeting the outer planet as a friend, and I think he gets the more creative edge of it. This is what I mean by crisis.

Now I would like to go on to the aspects of the outer planets in individual charts. I would first like to talk about what happens to the person who is tied intimately to the collective, and also about possible reasons why we have such great difficulty in accepting what the outer planets bring us. Natal aspects between inner planets and outer ones are almost impossible to be gracious about. They cause an endless amount of trouble. For example, you can consider an opposition between Venus and Pluto. That aspect has a very bad reputation in relationship matters. It's as though the person is a participant in a play where the director insists he play a part he doesn't personally like. With Venus-Pluto you are simply not allowed to live with others in a superficial way. You can meet someone when you're quite young, and think they're really nice and lovely, and you both fall in love and want to get married and settle down. Then you buy a nice house in a nice suburb and have 2.3 children and two cars and theoretically you should both live happily ever after. But if you see a signature like Venus-Pluto in your birth chart, there is no way that you're going to be able to get away with that. You are given a different fate. On a conscious level you might want security, contentment, peace and happiness. We all do. But those things will be shattered at some point, so that you can get a glimpse of the enormously complex inner world that underlies all that nice collectively acceptable domesticity. In other words, relationships will force you to deepen and become aware of darker and more powerful currents in yourself and in life. All relationships become a gateway to Pluto. So every time you allow anyone close to you, you invoke Pluto, and expose yourself to the experience of being changed and challenged and forced into your darker and less conscious emotional needs and drives. There is no way that can be avoided if you have Venus-Pluto, except to avoid intimate relationships, which is what many Venus-Pluto people tend to do.

I don't feel that Venus-Pluto is a bad aspect. What seems to make it behave badly is the refusal to allow this deeper level of experience into a relationship. I think it makes a difference if a person can accept this path as part of his life. Then he might have more chance to work with Pluto creatively, instead of being the planet's victim. Pluto doesn't have to destroy relationships, but he will certainly do that if you are very stubborn and pretend that everything can be solved by pleasant discussion or denial. If you are determined to keep everything peaceful and calm and do everything you can to avoid confrontations either with your partner or yourself, then of course Pluto will turn destructive, because instead of permitting the relationship to change you, you are then demanding that the relationship itself change. It usually does, in a devastating way. There is a tendency when this happens to blame the partner, but if it's the partner who walks out, you can be pretty sure it's the Venus-Pluto who has architected it.

Sometimes the need to destroy is experienced inside oneself. I think that's a progression upward from blaming the other person, but it's much harder to recognise that you are trying to kill something you love. It makes no sense, and goes against any rational reason or moral decency. Whether this leads in the end to staying or leaving isn't really the point. I think the point is to discover that emotions are often terribly ambivalent and that love is far more complicated than *Bride Magazine* is prepared to admit. The capacity to betray is one of Pluto's faces, and to find that you yourself are capable of betraying someone you love is pretty difficult if you have any idealism at all in matters of love. To discover that love can die is also an awful face of Pluto, because we want to believe that it's permanent if it's the real thing. Power battles and manipulation and cruelty and sexual control are other Plutonian favourites. Obviously a person with Venus in Aquarius opposite Pluto in Leo, or Venus in Taurus in square to Pluto, is not going to be very happy about all this because the conscious values are so much at odds with Pluto's primordial nature.

If you can somehow come to terms with throwing away your copy of *Bride Magazine* then that's a beginning. The experiences of Pluto become part and parcel of one's love life if he aspects Venus. Probably the hardest thing to live with under this aspect is the loneliness one feels in pursuing the strange underworld path. There aren't any collective guidelines, and the collective standards of one's world tend to be very intolerant of Pluto. Pluto is a loner, and it is a very lonely experience going down into the labyrinth to meet yourself. But that meeting offers depth and strength and a quality of love that is impossible to find in any other way. And I think it's a kind of fate.

This is an example of what happens when an inner planet contacts an outer one. A strange fate intrudes into an apparently ordinary personal sphere of life, and the individual is pulled into experiences which he usually feels he didn't ask for and certainly doesn't like. There is something rather archaic and impersonal about the outer planets, and we find ourselves behaving in ways that don't feel like our usual selves. This is why they can be very frightening. One gets a glimpse of something that has the power of a god, and collective consciousness can't help because its rules are quite ineffectual. This is part of the reason why outer planets are often painful and disagreeable. One must find completely different values and standards to deal with them, and that means separating from the comforting shelter of conventional codes. These codes are as much inner as outer, and don't just mean rules about sexual behaviour. Inner conventional codes tell us it's right or wrong to feel certain things or want certain things, whether this is acted out or not.

An aspect such as sun conjunct Neptune is not in itself a bad aspect, anymore than Venus opposite Pluto is bad. Nor is it good. It's simply there. Charts don't moralise and say this is a good or a bad quality to have. They make no statements of that kind. We tack our morals onto astrology, but the planets and signs make no comment. They merely suggest that this is your piece of cosmos for a lifetime, and you must make of it what you can. The sun conjuncting Neptune suggests that the issue of individuality, of becoming oneself, gets bound up with the longing for the mystical union and the dissolving of individual boundaries. To put it in the form of truism, the person must lose himself in order to find himself. There is a constant conflict between the sun and Neptune, because they pull in different directions. But if they're in conjunction, then ultimately they are going to try to create an individual who is both himself and who can be open to the larger whole of which he is a part. In a sense, that person has an open door from the personal level down to the collective unconscious level. All of the longings and yearnings and dreams and visions of his collective seep through into his own feeling life, and he is irresistibly attracted to those movements where these longings can find a place.

A person with sun-Neptune can't escape this fate, although I think many people with this aspect will try to shut out Neptune. The longing for something ineffable and the sense of the world's suffering are very real things for Neptunian people, and they can be felt as a terrible threat because they imply a disintegration of the personality. Neptune identifies with the figure of the victim, and generally feels that the world is a pretty awful place and can he please go home soon. One of the things which I think can plague sun-Neptune is the uneasy remembering of where one comes from, the place where there wasn't any conflict or suffering or struggle to be an individual alone in the world. But these fantasies are not just personal ones, and it would be a mistake to reduce them to a longing for mother's womb. They are a deep religious urge in the collective, to which the sun-Neptune person is privy. So he must somehow find a way to combine his own talents and goals with these collective longings, because he's a mediator of them for the group.

I once did a chart for a woman with the sun in the first house opposite Neptune in the seventh. She was a rather sad person, because she felt she had never been able to have anything in life she really wanted. Her father had been an alcoholic, and much of her childhood had been spent avoiding scenes in the household between her parents. Her mother had been a very practical, managing woman, who of course blamed the weak father for everything. My client eventually married a nice, promising young man, but an ill fate seemed to dog her, because after a couple of years of marriage the husband became alcoholic. The woman divorced this man, and a few years later married again. The second husband again turned out to be alcoholic. It finally began to dawn on her that something was at work in her life that was beyond her control. She was a lot like her mother in that she felt the way to get things one wants is to dominate everybody in sight until they cough up the goods. She became very frightened when she saw this pattern at work. As Ian Fleming once wrote, "Once is chance, twice is coincidence, and three times is enemy action."

The opposition of the sun and Neptune certainly placed a fate on this woman, but I don't think it was that she was doomed to spend her life with alcoholic men. Somehow she managed to throw off the inner responsibility which sun-Neptune required of her. Admittedly it isn't an easy aspect to try to live, not least because ordinary social standards run against all the things Neptune represents. But my client was too frightened of the dissolution and entry into the magical world that I think Neptune requires, so she projected her Neptune on her partners. This is to be expected when it is in the seventh house. The alcoholic father described by sun-Neptune is not just an alcoholic. He is a distorted symbol of someone thirsting for the spirit, and I did mean that as a pun. But there is a close connection between the kind of alcoholic who drinks to find some magical or transcendent reality and the mystic who is also looking for the same experience of losing himself in the divine. My client's sun-Neptune describes an inheritance from the father, which is a deep spiritual thirst. She couldn't accommodate this with her conscious personality, which was very practical. So she rejected the father, and found husbands who enacted the same Neptunian tendencies in the same negative way.

What this woman did is what most of us habitually do with outer planet aspects. We tend to project them into rather distorted forms. Neptune materialises as the alcoholic or the deceitful partner, and Uranus dresses as the partner who leaves you, and Pluto disguises himself as the partner who has power over you or has some pretty complicated sexual and emotional patterns. But I think it's possible to at least try to live these things in one's own life. That can be exhilarating and creative, if we can come to terms with the fear. The child with strong outer planet aspects tends to be singled out when he's young. He's usually the one the other children think is a little weird. He may suffer from a lot of collective pressure in the form of conventional expectations, especially if the outer planet is in a prominent place like the ascendant or the midheaven. Because this child answers to a different drumbeat, he is often avoided by his soberer fellows who have aspects like sun-Saturn and sun-Jupiter and sun-Mars and are better adapted to the social order. A person with strong outer planet contacts may have a disruptive effect in the group, because the outer planets tend to feel threatening to more Saturnian values. Sometimes you can see the opposite extreme to the woman I just described. The person may get so used to having strangeness projected onto him that he begins to identify wholly with the outer planet. Then he becomes the anarchist or the dropout or the renegade against the social order. In pursuing this path to the extreme he loses the sun, which means he no longer has a sense of his own individual values. He is nothing but a mouthpiece for the collective unconscious, and he can be very destructive not only to others but also to himself.

Outer planet aspects aren't the easiest things to carry. I think they require a lot of insight. In some ways it's fortunate if the outer planets aren't too active in the horoscope, because you have a better chance for a relatively comfortable, placid and uneventful life. A lot of people value this highly, and I don't think it should be sneered at. Jung suggests that the unconscious should be left alone unless it starts knocking at the door, and if you are well adapted to ordinary life and have good relationships with other people and aren't in wild pursuit of some other-worldly vision, that doesn't mean you're "unevolved." It just means you're sound. But if you have a dominant outer planet in the chart then you must come to terms with it. I think one place to start is to see where it might be projected.

Audience: Does this apply to the sun and moon?

Liz: I think it applies to everything in the chart. We don't only project the outer planets. We also project many other bits of ourselves. It's just that the outer planets are much harder to recognise as "mine." They aren't really "mine" or "yours." They're an "it," and it's better if one preserves that sense of separateness while still recognising that they operate in one's personal life. If the sun is the thing which is projected, then I think this means the person has no clear sense of himself and his own individual values. He's a collective creature in the ordinary sense, which means a mouthpiece for conventional social opinions and values. Or he may be a creature dominated by the deeper unconscious collective, in the form of the outer planets. But either way he hasn't got a strong ego, a strong sense of his own person. That becomes his task, and he may rely on others to provide the feeling of individuality in his life.

If the moon is projected, then I think the person is very disassociated from his feeling needs. He isn't aware of being related to others, and may rely on someone else to do his feeling for him. I won't run through all the planets because I think you can work this out for yourselves. But I have found that it's typical, maybe inevitable that we project the outer planets. Perhaps we always will, and can only accommodate a very little bit of what they might mean. I think it becomes dangerous when we're completely devoid of awareness of them, which is when they behave like blind fate.

I would like to talk now about what happens when Saturn gets mixed up with the outer planets. The conjunctions of Saturn with Uranus, Neptune and Pluto represent a group of people all born within two or two and a half years of each other. They are a kind of small generation group. Not everyone has Saturn conjunct an outer planet. The squares, trines and oppositions work in similar ways, but I will talk mainly about the conjunctions because they're much more obvious. From around May 1941 to April 1943 Saturn and Uranus were conjuncting. They started off in Taurus and they continued to conjunct in the first decanate of Gemini. This is a two-year generation group. Saturn and Uranus will be conjuncting again at the end of 1986 for around two years, starting in Sagittarius and moving into Capricorn. They also conjuncted at the end of the last century. There are usually two or three of these conjunctions during the course of a century.

There was a Saturn-Neptune conjunction in Libra from the end of 1951 to the end of 1953. There was another between 1916 and 1918. There will be a final conjunction of Saturn and Neptune this century between 1988 and 1990. There have been two Saturn-Pluto conjunctions this century, one between 1915 and 1917 and another from the autumn of 1946 through the end of 1948. And there will be a third between January 1982 and the beginning of 1984. This gives you an idea of the cyclical nature of the conjunctions. They tend to occur around forty years apart with each outer planet. Sometimes they overlap, which is the case in the late 1980's when the Saturn-Uranus conjunction meets the Saturn-Neptune conjunction.

I mentioned before that the major movements which arise from the deep collective layers of the psyche run into Saturn first on their way out into life. Saturn is the natural barrier of the ego, the defensive aspect of the ego which tries to preserve its autonomy and its separateness. People who have Saturn aspecting the outer planets tend to feel the impact of collective currents very strongly, and in an uncomfortable way, because there is an urgency to anchor them in order to render them safe. Saturn is concerned with building forms to contain chaotic energies. So a person with Saturn-Uranus must do something with the new ideas that are flooding into his awareness. It isn't enough for him just to be forward-looking and eccentric and unconventional, which might be sufficient for sun-Uranus. Saturn-Uranus has the responsibility of actually constructing some vehicle, because otherwise he will feel perpetually threatened and anxious. I think it's important to remember that Saturn rules Capricorn and the tenth house, and is concerned with the public arena of the world. Saturn-Uranus is in the curious position of having to do something in the world with his social or political vision, but without either losing his sense of realism and worldly wisdom or crushing the vision into a too conventional framework. That's a pretty delicate balance, and you usually find that the person is tipping to one extreme or the other, and finding his enemy "out there" in society as either the violently anarchistic Uranus or the oppressive authoritarian Saturn.

With Saturn-Neptune, it isn't sufficient to simply pursue the mystic's path, or become an artist or a musician and give voice to the images from the depths. Saturn-Neptune must make Neptune work in the world in some way, and that's even more difficult than Saturn-Uranus because Neptune's diffuse vision of inclusive love is very far away from earthy Saturnian reality. The dream of the utopian society is a very urgent vision for many Saturn-Neptune people, and they try to implement it by forming alternative social structures such as communes or esoteric groups. As with Saturn-Uranus, it's difficult to stand in the middle, and much more common to tip to either extreme. Either the material world is condemned as crass and unspiritual, or the mystical world is condemned as irresponsible and degenerate.

Saturn-Pluto puts a person in touch with the necessity for endings. Either he must perpetrate the destruction of something in society, or he must facilitate its transformation. He carries the responsibility of finding a place for the primordial instincts in the world, which means that he has to face both the deep transformative power of the instincts and also their savagery. Very often Saturn-Pluto becomes a saboteur, working toward toppling some entrenched structure or set of values. In many ways he may find himself the enemy of everything patriarchal, where emotions and instincts have been suppressed for too long. Or he may fly to the opposite extreme, and fight the instincts in a very tyrannical way. Saturn-Pluto is a very compulsive and obsessive combination, because Pluto is a raw force of nature with the most tremendous power. It's not surprising that many Saturn-Pluto people are rather paranoid, and fear the destructive power of the mass as well as the destructive power of their own emotional depths.

Obviously if you are quite young these Saturn contacts with the outer planets can be terribly uncomfortable and frightening. Many people have some form of breakdown early in life, because the ego isn't yet strong enough to give shape to the energies pushing in from the unconscious. Of course we are given absolutely no education about these things, so a person who is being driven a little wild by the pressure of the outer planets is often treated in a very uncomprehending way. The critical factor seems to be the strength and health of the ego. One of the ways in which the pressure shows itself is in a tremendous affinity with causes. Outer planet contacts with Saturn tend to reflect a propensity for joining movements in a rather fanatical way. Or sometimes you see the opposite, where the individual feels himself to be the personal enemy of such movements, as though it were his sole responsibility for stamping them out. If the person is frightened enough of the impact of the outer planets, he can take the role of Saturn and try to repress all the Uranian, Neptunian and Plutonian elements in society.

Naturally, not every single person with Saturn conjunct Uranus, Neptune or Pluto will feel the same way and do the same thing. Probably it depends on how strongly the conjunction is placed in the horoscope. The house placement matters, and so do the aspects to other planets. I think the conjunctions represent a responsibility that belongs to a particular generation group, and that group will elect mouthpieces who give voice to its meaning. Many people with these conjunctions are quite unconscious of them, but there is a pressure that builds up from the group and it bursts out through the mouths of the spokesmen.

I spent quite a bit of time thinking about the Saturn-Uranus group born between 1941 and 1943. What happened to them? Who are they? What has this group done with its conjunction? The first thing that occurred to me was that this group really formed the bedrock of the whole hippie generation. One of the earliest voices of the enormous cultural movement that has changed so many things in the last couple of decades was Bob Dylan, who is one of the Saturn-Uranus group. I think the words from one of his songs expresses nicely the sentiments which began to break through: "You'd better start swimming or you'll sink like a stone/ For the times they are a-changin'." Dylan and Joan Baez and the Beatles formed the vanguard of a movement that expressed a political ideology through music. This I think is appropriate for Saturn conjunct Uranus in trine to Neptune. The music-politics combination was more than just fashionable. It changed lifestyles in an irrevocable way. Morals and religious attitudes and relationships with one's country were turned about completely. It would be hard to overestimate the yeasting effect of these people. The Beatles brought a funny little Indian man who called himself the Maharishi into public prominence, and lo and behold, everyone began meditating. Many things which have now become virtually respectable were for this group initially heretical and iconoclastic. Not only was this Saturn-Uranus group giving voice to an ideology, it was also expressing the imagery and spiritual sentiments of Neptune. I think this is why the particular combination of politics, drugs and music had such an effect.

Obviously Bob Dylan is not the only way to explain a Saturn-Uranus conjunction. But he's a good example. The thing which is most characteristic is not that a singer became popular. That happens all the time. It's that a few people expressed attitudes which spread like a bush fire. When someone symbolises something that the collective has secretly been striving toward without realising it, then that person has enormous influence.

I'm much vaguer about the current Saturn-Neptune group. At the moment they are just beginning to experience the Saturn return, and I'm not at all sure what they will do. I talked earlier about the urge to anchor some mystical or spiritual vision in society, and I'm sure the products of this group will develop along those lines. I know a bit more about the Saturn-Pluto group born just after World War Two because they had their Saturn return a couple of years ago, and that period just after the Saturn return seems to be the most popular time for visiting an astrologer. I'm not sure why, unless it's that one has come to terms with certain things under the Saturn return, and then there is a period of re-orientation when the person sits about wondering which way to go next.

The peculiarities of Saturn-Pluto have struck me as particularly interesting because of the frequency of what a psychotherapist would call "symptoms" such as claustrophobia. I began inquiring more deeply into these things with my Saturn-Pluto clients. One of the first things that emerged was an almost universal hatred of crowds. The experience of panic in crowds seems surprisingly common among this group. As you might expect of a conjunction like this in Leo, there isn't an overwhelming love of authority either, but this goes deeper than the usual father-problem. It seems to be a real hatred of any figurehead who has the power to influence the mass. I have seen a very strong anarchistic streak in Saturn-Pluto, which expresses as a desire to destroy. Often the object of destruction is unclear, but it's usually someone or something in authority.

I think there is a lot of violence inherent in the Saturn-Pluto conjunction. This may be expressed on a physical or an emotional level, but either way the responses are closer to jungle law than to so-called civilised behaviour. Obviously this is hard to take in oneself if the rest of the chart is very gentle or refined or controlled. There also seems to be a fierce isolation expressed by Saturn-Pluto. I have found when teaching groups that the Saturn-Pluto people don't like to be considered one of the group. The whole feeling of "group" in the popular Aquarian sense is highly irritating to many Saturn-Pluto people. They tend to enroll in a seminar or workshop and lurk about in the back and take what they want from it and then leave, but they won't "share" according to humanistic psychological jargon. They don't think of themselves as members of a group.

I have also found that you cannot push Saturn-Pluto people. I think there have been many problems among this group with early education, because the moment you attempt to impose any ideology on them, or assert any kind of control, you get a very perverse and very violent reaction. Naturally the degree of this varies, just as the degree of political iconoclasm varies in Saturn-Uranus. Some Saturn-Pluto people are much more obvious in their hatred of imposed restrictions. I think this expresses what I mentioned before about Pluto being the enemy of patriarchal systems and laws. You can reach Saturn-Pluto through feeling, but you cannot reach it through authority. Mars came along during 1948 and met up with the Saturn-Pluto conjunction, and this particular section of the group is understandably much more overtly angry, although the anger and aggression may be unconscious.

There is one more curious thing about this conjunction which runs deeper than behaviour patterns. I have met with a number of Saturn-Pluto people whose dream material throws up frequent images of the last World War. These often focus on the theme of the concentration camp, and on the German-Jewish dilemma. The first time I met with this kind of imagery I worked with it in terms of the individual's experiences. But after I encountered it a few times I became increasingly curious about it. The Saturn-Pluto conjunction in Leo occurred after the war had ended, and therefore cannot be a direct childhood memory or experience. But the feeling of it is *as though* this group had a direct experience of the horror of the Holocaust. Now we can get into a huge argument about whether this demonstrates reincarnation at work, but I am not really interested in that because there is no way we will ever know. But I am very interested in the Holocaust as a symbol. The core of the imagery is the issue of persecutor and persecuted, which is embodied in the Nazi hunting the Jew. We must ask what the figure of the scapegoat means, and what this might represent in society. The scapegoat is the dark, rejected, shadowy side of man, and the image of the blonde German superman attempting to root out the dark Jewish "inferior" man is really a very archaic mythic theme. In some way the problem of Saturn-Pluto is about an attempt to reconcile these two sides of life, and the inner conflict can be very violent because I think the Saturn-Pluto person has both a Hitler and a persecuted scapegoat inside him.

Most of these Saturn-Pluto people whom I questioned are neither German nor Jewish, so it can hardly be an issue of racial allegiances. I have also met the same themes among the earlier Saturn-Pluto group who were born during the First World War, and they of course did not absorb Holocaust themes in childhood as the later group might have done. But these people have told me some very funny things. They say, "Yes, I have a recurrent dream of being in a gas chamber." One individual said, "Whenever I get into a crowded bus or subway I start fantasising soldiers coming in." Although these images are cloaked in modern dress, the theme is not new. It's an ancient one, and I might go so far as to say that the responsibility falls on the Saturn-Pluto group to find some resolution of this terrible split between the light face of civilisation and the dark face of the primitive man. No one feels that split more acutely than Saturn-Pluto.

Of course the more esoterically inclined can say that the Saturn-Pluto people born between 1946 and 1948 simply reincarnated in rather a hurry and really did experience the Holocaust. But that explanation, although it might be a valid one, doesn't really describe the psychological importance of the conjunction, or what it might be for in a creative sense. Certainly it feels to Saturn-Pluto as though the person really did experience the war, but I understand this to mean that the person contains within himself a particular quality of conflict which the war also embodied. Perhaps these people may have something to say about whether such a thing will ever happen again.

More than anyone else I think the Saturn-Pluto group has a deeper understanding of what that war was really about. Saturn-Pluto mistrusts mass psychology for some very valid reasons. We tend to see the last war as a political problem, brought about by a dictator who wanted Germany to rule the world. But it's much subtler than that. There are lots of ways to rule a world, without necessarily having to engage in hunting scapegoats or "inferior races." That is a psychological phenomenon of a group casting its shadow on another group to avoid the experience of its own evil, and it's a problem that is not limited to wartime Germany.

I have had the feeling for a long time that Pluto symbolises an archaic feminine power which has been excluded from religious worship for a very long time. I think Pluto has many connections with the Great Mother who was revered all over the Middle East and the Mediterranean as the goddess of fertility and death. She has been particularly repressed among those countries in northern Europe, who have always worshipped a sky-god. In Aeschylos' trilogy, the *Oresteia*, the Furies are outraged because Mother-right has been violated, and they inflict punishment and madness on Orestes. I have a fantasy that the Goddess has become quite outraged at her neglect, and her revenge is the kind of eruption of madness we witnessed forty years ago. This is what I believe rose to the surface under the guise of Naziism. I cannot think in terms of it being the "fault" of the Germans. Perhaps the German nation was a weak link because it was in such a state of internal collapse. An individual who is in a very low and disintegrated state is much more prone to invasion by the unconscious. Perhaps also the collective background of Germany made it a likely vessel because the Teutonic peoples always gave precedence to a male deity, and never worshipped the Mother as the Mediterranean cultures did. That would mean that there was little or no real understanding or integration of the feminine, and therefore no way of coping with its angrier face. They were simply taken over. But this might have happened anywhere. It would be a mistake to blame the Holocaust on political principles.

My feeling is that Pluto, the Dark Mother, erupted in rage and violence through a particular political entity which gave her a vehicle. Until the rise of the Third Reich we liked to think of ourselves in the West as essentially civilised and moral. Then we were shocked at the cruelty and atrocity of something which we still persist in believing was exclusively the property of the Germans. But I think the problem lies closer to home. Until a person can face those forces in himself and make some sense of what is happening, then he will continue to project his Pluto on races and nations. I think the enactment of the last war is really an individual issue. You can see so many individuals still obsessed with it. I

don't just mean concern with what happened; I mean the existence of a Neo-Nazi party in many countries, including America.
The motifs and imagery of the Holocaust exercise a queer fascination on us all. They are profound symbols of an internal collision.

I suppose I have the fantasy that the people who are born with
Saturn in strong aspect to Pluto have some particular individual
issue to understand about all this, and perhaps also some responsibility in the outer world because they are better placed to understand it in themselves. There seems to be quite a lot of honesty, at
least self-honesty, in that Saturn-Pluto group, and I have heard
many of them express their concern and fear because they are
aware of a particular violence or sexual cruelty in themselves. I
suspect that this violence is not exclusive to Saturn-Pluto, but
rather that Saturn-Pluto cannot avoid seeing it and feeling the
necessity of understanding it and trying to work with it. I think
maybe that is their contribution to the collective.

Audience: Don't you think this is a reincarnation idea? I have
had what I thought were reincarnation dreams, and in one of
them I finished up in a concentration camp in Germany in the
last war and was actually living during that time. As far as I know
it could have been an experience of reincarnation. I have no other
explanation for this.

Liz: That's why I'm trying to approach it psychologically. I'm not
quarrelling with the idea of reincarnation, but I think your dream
has a symbolic inner meaning as well. For you to be in a concentration camp says something about how you might feel in your
life now. Whether it also means you literally were in a camp
doesn't alter that. Do you have a Saturn-Pluto aspect?

Audience: Yes, I have a Saturn-Pluto opposition.

Liz: I really don't know about the metaphysical side of all this.
Different people believe different things. The one thing I am
pretty certain of is that such an image means something to the
person as he is in the present life. It's a psychological statement.
They're not mutually exclusive. One could argue that you have
a tendency to feel victimised and persecuted by authority figures
because you had a bad past life experience. That's as may be. But
the reality is that you feel that way now, and your dream states it

very baldly. I would be more interested in what side of you the Germans represented, and why a state of internal persecution existed between two different aspects of you, than I would be interested in whether you were really alive in 1943. That won't help you now.

If you really want to get a strong taste of what Saturn-Pluto feels like, then you must look at the images of the last war, because the last war is a paradigm of Saturn-Pluto. It's a powerful symbol of what I feel this aspect is about, including the overwhelming Plutonian dictatorship and the crushed scapegoat that is hunted and persecuted, which is also in a strange way Plutonian. All the sexual sadism and dreams of racial purity and supermen are bound up with Saturn-Pluto. Watching Wagnerian opera is an education in Saturn-Pluto as well.

Oddly, Israel was born as a state under that same Saturn-Pluto conjunction that followed the Holocaust. This is either a piece of immense cosmic irony, or it's something very profound. Unfortunately the behaviour of this very great and dedicated new nation sometimes verges horribly close to the very thing that engendered its birth.* This suggests something very paradoxical, which Jung called *enantiodromia*. That means that if you polarise very violently against an opposite, you have a tendency to secretly become that opposite without realising it. I feel this is the danger of polarising with any of the outer planet conjunctions with Saturn. If you fight too hard against one side, you wind up being taken over by it unconsciously. The same danger lies in Saturn-Uranus and Saturn-Neptune. If Saturn tries to fight too hard against Neptunian idealism and romanticism by attempting to be incredibly practical, it tends to secretly behave like a religious fanatic bringing the kingdom of heaven down to earth, without even being aware of its messianic aura. It works the other way, too. Saturn-Uranus may polarise on the Uranian side and talk about freedom and change of the educational system and overthrowing of conventional authority, but unconsciously it will be as authoritarian and rigid and tyrannical as the very thing it kicks against. You can see what a tremendous challenge aspects like these are to the individual.

---

*This comment was made in reference to the situation in the Middle East in 1980. The present situation between Israel and the Palestinians in the summer of 1982 tends to make me wish to repeat that comment even more forcibly.

I think a good historical paradigm of Saturn-Uranus is the French Revolution, just as the last war is a good paradigm of Saturn-Pluto. The French Revolution was spawned by an idea, or three to be precise—liberty, equality, fraternity. It was supposed to provide these noble ideals for everybody, by overthrowing the effete monarchy. It ended in a bloodbath which was the complete antithesis of liberty, equality and fraternity, and after all that effort another dictator eventually took control in the form of Napoleon. These things just don't seem to work very well when we try to act them out in society. They have to be dealt with in the individual.

Audience: What is the difference between an idea and a myth?

Liz: I suppose they often overlap. But to me an idea is something conceptual and abstract. Liberty, equality and fraternity are concepts of a particular kind of social relationship. The myth of Prometheus who brings fire to mankind has some of the same feeling, but it's a spontaneous image which people don't think about. It arises from the unconscious as a compelling image, but the intellectual content is hidden in the image. I think Uranian ideas often have a myth embedded in them, but people usually think they are being enlightened and rational when they perpetrate an idea. The myth is translated by the thinking function into something recognisable in space and time. The ideological content of the French Revolution began with the observation that the peasants were being oppressed. The ideas of the Revolution were believed to be rational, reasonable, fair and possible. There are many myths where someone oppressed or imprisoned is set free, often with violence. But no Greek would have claimed that the story of Zeus and his brothers and sisters overthrowing the tyranny of their father Kronos was an idea for the perfect Greek state. It was a religious statement about what the Greeks believed to be the gods or ruling powers of the cosmos. A group of people will sit down and discuss an idea. You cannot sit and discuss a myth like that. You simply experience it as something alive and numinous.

Myth bursts into life in ways that are nonrational. Much of the Nazi myth burst out in Wagner's Siegfried. I don't think anyone, particularly Wagner himself, could have sat down with a cigarette and a brandy and said to himself, "I have this great idea for a new

German state." Wagner didn't make Siegfried. Siegfried possessed Wagner, and after Wagner he possessed Germany. Much later, when everyone had got properly possessed, then people began to come up with ideas about nationalising industry and restoring German pride and purifying the race. I don't know. Perhaps Uranian ideas are vehicles for myths which communicate themselves in a form which people think is rational.

I think sometimes one can have an idea and in order to propogate that idea myths can be drawn on. I'll give you an obscure historical example. In the early seventeenth century a man called Friedrich, the Elector-Palatine—which means one of several German princes ruling over a small chunk of the Austrian Empire— tried to make himself King of Bohemia. He did this to challenge the Catholic rule of the Habsburgs, and to allow a country where Protestants could enjoy freedom of worship. He and his followers believed in an idea, which wasn't a new one but which meant a lot to Friedrich. He promoted his idea by utilising myth. He was involved with the founding of the Rosicrucian Brotherhood, which began spreading the myth of the invisible elite of spiritual initiates who guided the affairs of ordinary men. This is an ancient myth, and it shouldn't surprise those of you who have only come upon it in Alice Bailey or Theosophy. Friedrich had the idea of a spiritually enlightened state where all could enjoy their own forms of worship. This was an anomaly in Habsburg-controlled Catholic Europe. Of course he got stamped out. But it was a nice idea, and good politicians have always known the value of backing up Uranus with Neptune.

Apropos Uranus and Neptune, I think Marxism is an interesting example of the combination of idea and myth, or perhaps the combination of ideology and religion. Marxism is as much a religion as it is a political system, although typically the dedicated Marxist considers himself above religion which is only the opiate of the masses. Marx himself was born under a Uranus-Neptune conjunction in Sagittarius. Although I run the risk of angering any Marxists in the group, I think Marxism is as mystical as Rosicrucianism. The Perfect State is an ancient myth, and one of its oldest symbols is the Heavenly Jerusalem. The passionate belief in the State is not very distinguishable from the passionate belief in the Heavenly Jerusalem. But it poses as an idea, because there is a rational content to Marxism which is not present in mystical Christianity.

There are a great many ideas or systems of ideas which have a hidden religious content. I think there is a strong flavour of this in much of Freud's psychoanalytic theory. Freud rejected God, but he raised the instincts to the status of a deity. Freud's *id* is not really very far away from the Yahveh of his Jewish ancestors, who is all-powerful and attempts to exact obedience. There is a religious feeling in the psychoanalytic movement as much as there is a religious feeling in Marxism. Both pretend to be wholly rational. The mystical content may in the end be more valid to the individual than the ideological content. But most systems of ideas are very ashamed of admitting any traffick with the mystical or mythical.

Audience: Something that strikes me is that Russia's present position in the world seems to tie up with the two Saturn-Pluto conjunctions you mentioned. The Russian Revolution occurred during the first conjunction and the rise of Russia as an important world power occurred during the second one.

Liz: I was going to put up Russia's chart tomorrow so that we could discuss it, so I would rather leave that until later. The idea was to show that the same principles that work within an individual's psyche also operate within the psyche of a nation. In Russia's horoscope in fact there is a Saturn-Neptune conjunction in Leo opposite Uranus in Aquarius. This horoscope is based on the time that the Bolshevik party took power. But we can go into it in more detail tomorrow.

Lecture Three

I would like to begin today with some example charts of famous persons where the outer planets seem to be a key of some kind to the individual's motivations. I don't mean by this that the outer planets, or anything else in the horoscope for that matter, will describe such things as genius or greatness for good or evil. It is very easy to take a chart such as that of Hitler, which is one of the ones I want to discuss, and try to see from it why he was able to acquire the power he did. But I don't think the chart will tell us that. Without hindsight you could not really have estimated what this man became. Also, there were many babies born around the same time as Hitler. But a psychological portrait is possible from the chart, and in particular I am going to look for any propensity for being open to and channelling or being a vehicle for collective influences. I don't think one can look at Hitler's chart, or Marx's, which is the other one I want to discuss, and tell from the natal horoscope that these men would have the effect they had on history. But it's their sensitivity to history that will show, by which I mean their receptivity to the collective currents of their times. This kind of receptivity can of course come out in very different ways. It might drive one person completely mad, it might express in another through an artistic medium, it might manifest in a third as a political talent, and in a fourth it might never express at all but would provide a very potent psychic atmosphere which eventually infiltrates the person's children and affects the course of their lives. But I think that both Hitler and Marx are very good modern examples of men who became lenses for movements that erupted out of the collective, irregardless of any moral judgment we might have on the rightness or wrongness of those movements.

The outer planets in this horoscope, or in any other, will not tell the astrologer whether they are going to express in a "right" or a "wrong" way. If there is such a thing as morality in the unconscious, it is the morality of nature, not that of our civilised egos. Probably whether someone decides to behave, or is compelled to behave, in a socially appropriate or inappropriate fashion depends a great deal on the state of consciousness of the individual who is experiencing these collective energies. I think we must

consider them amoral. Sometimes things serve an evolutionary
purpose or a function in individual development or social development which everything in us declares is immoral. But I
would not like to make a judgment. In Hitler's chart there is a
Pluto-Neptune conjunction placed in Gemini in the eighth house.
This conjunction receives no major aspects from other planets,
which I feel is a very important point. Uranus is placed right on
the ascendant. In Marx's chart there is a Neptune-Uranus conjunction. This conjunction is in square to Saturn and Pluto. These
are the particular configurations in the two charts that I would
like to discuss now.

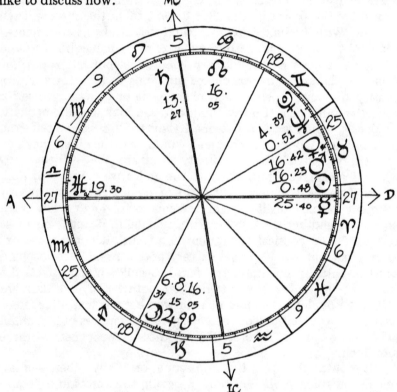

Illustration 2: BIRTH CHART OF ADOLPH HITLER
April 20, 1889, 6:30 PM, Braunau, Austria
Source: Howe, <u>Astrology, A Recent History,</u>
"Baptismal records in Braunau".

Pluto and Neptune in the eighth house and Uranus in the twelfth in Hitler's chart suggest to me a marked receptivity to ideas and movements percolating on a deeply hidden level. Because Uranus is very concerned with ideologies, its position here implies that Hitler was peculiarly vulnerable to any new political movements that might be lurking around during his lifetime. This doesn't say that he would be inclined to "good" or "bad" political movements. I think the key to what he picked up lies in the state of Germany after the First World War, because Germany was in a state of collapse and disintegration and the time was ripe for something to come bursting out. Hitler's chart doesn't make him a Nazi, but it suggests that if the thing we call Naziism is floating around, this man would resonate to it like a tuning fork. Uranus is opposite Mercury, so here again is the suggestion of someone whose thinking and perceptions are going to be strongly coloured by those ideological movements which are not quite ready to manifest fully into society. The direction of Hitler's ideas in his youth was already firmly set and borne along by the new currents, long before the country as a whole was prepared to take them seriously. So the placement of Uranus simply tells us that here is a political animal, with a political vision that was not really thought out as his own but which more or less "appeared" in his mind full-blown, because he was drawing it from the unconscious psyche of his collective. There is of course nothing strange about this aspect, you can find it in a lot of people's charts. Usually when I find Uranus placed like this in the twelfth house, there is a very strong interest in political movements and ideologies, but it is in a rather compulsive as opposed to reflective way.

The Pluto-Neptune conjunction on the other hand is rather strange, especially because of its lack of aspects. These two planets don't conjunct very often. When a planet is unaspected in a chart, it is a kind of unconscious pocket in the psyche. It is a drive or impulse which does not really relate to anything else in the person's life. Often he doesn't even know it's there, until it's triggered by a transit or a progression or by something in someone else's chart. It's as though there is a god who has no ordinary outlet in the life of the individual, so that it cannot accommodate itself to external life in a gradual way. It remains primordial and unpolished, full of tremendous energy which has no outlet. It just sits there and builds up steam. An unaspected planet is very raw and archaic. It has no social graces, but behaves as though it had just been let out of a very old prison. You can see this principle at work with unaspected inner planets as well. Often there is a kind of blank place, and the individual is sometimes very ignorant of that side of himself until it erupts. I suppose a very simple analogy would be that of the owner of a house which has an unknown tenant in the basement. The tenant has always been there, but the occupant has no idea of his existence. Occasionally there is a knock or two at night, in one's dreams, but otherwise it's very quiet. The occupant doesn't even know there is a basement in the house, let alone someone living in it. Then one day the tenant decides to emerge, so he suddenly throws open the door to the living room, or equally frequently, just crashes through the floorboards, and then he has to be reckoned with. And sometimes he takes possession of the entire house, and ties up the occupant helplessly in a chair.

When the unaspected planet is an outer planet, then it is in many ways much more critical, because it's so difficult to establish a dialogue with something collective. It can seem so potent and alien. An unaspected Venus which erupts may plunge the person into compulsive erotic or emotional states, but eventually these can be accommodated into his life. But Neptune and Pluto are too archetypal, too mythical. This conjunction in Hitler's chart is not likely to be easily integrated through a creative medium. And a little reflection on the state of the personal planets in the chart suggests that there are many areas of personal blockage and hurt and negativity that would make it doubly difficult to integrate something so powerful. What is likely to happen is that the grandiose mythic vision of Pluto-Neptune feeds into the personal feelings of inferiority and rejection and infantility of the Mars-Venus in square to Saturn, and swells it up like a toad. I think it is very much like what in medieval times would have been called a state of possession.

I don't mean this in a literal demonic sense, because Pluto and Neptune are not inherently evil. But in a psychological sense, something unconscious and very potent swamps the ego and takes control. It overwhelms the ego and floods in and takes over, twisting all the personal energies to its own ends. This is psychological possession. One of the more lurid examples of this in psychiatric literature is the situation of multiple personality, where the autonomous psychic images are completely disconnected from each other and take turns in expressing through the person's mouth. This is common enough, although less flamboyant, in cases of hysterical dissociation, where the person cannot remember the giddy, giggling, volatile person he was fifteen minutes ago, or where he goes on a drinking binge and then cannot remember anything at all—not only of what he said or did—but of why he even began it in the first place.

In all these cases something in the unconscious breaks through the barrier and takes possession of the ego. If a person is relatively aware, it is tormenting, because it's experienced as a terrible compulsion. Or he may develop amnesia about it, or let it just disappear altogether. When it's an outer planet, then the thing that floods in is something very collective. There is a film called *The Triumph of the Will*, which was made as a propaganda film by the Nazi party, which is a rather terrifying visual enactment of what I am talking about. You can see Hitler preparing to give a speech to an audience. He stands rather diffidently in the background, obviously unsure of himself, very eager to please. He climbs up to the podium, and smiles and dimples and shuffles a bit. You can see the Libra ascendant in all this shuffling and shyness and fear that people won't like him. He begins to speak in a fairly ordinary voice. Then something begins to happen. His gestures change completely and begin to become rather jerky, and his voice alters, and his eyes glaze over. You can see the tenant in the basement rising up to take control of the house. All of a sudden this rather shy and diffident man begins to radiate immense charismatic power. He is giving voice to what everyone in the audience is caught by. They are all in a state of *participation mystique*, and the collective vision has taken possession of them all.

Neptune, as I mentioned before, is connected with dreams and religious longings; the yearning for return to the source. Pluto is connected with the urge for destruction and renewal, the tearing down of the old world order so that something new might be born. If you put these two principles together, what you have is essentially a religious or mystical movement which is dedicated to the destruction and rebuilding of society. I think this is very literally what Hitler attempted to perpetrate as the vision of National Socialism. He was the figurehead for a tremendous dictatorial-mystical cult. The Pluto side of it says something like, "The new world must be created. The old one must be utterly annihilated, and all elements which taint or spoil it must be destroyed." The Neptune side says, "The new superman is God's chosen vessel. He is the vessel for the light. He is the embodiment of God on earth, and rules by sacred right." This conjunction is bumping around here unaspected in the eighth house. So when it erupts, it is likely to do so in a completely uncontrolled way, because there is nothing in the chart to help channel it.

Hitler was part of the fabric of his time, and was a mouthpiece for the Pluto-Neptune conjunction. No doubt there were other mouthpieces as well, some of a much more creative and beneficent kind. But he met the requirements of his time. I think it is a mistake to make him responsible for them. There were a good many civilised and liberal-minded Englishmen and Frenchmen who thought at first that he might be able to do something really constructive in Germany, because this mystical vision of rebuilding society was around in the collective, not just in Hitler. This conjunction occurred everywhere, not just in Germany. Japan and Italy polarised with Germany, but they could not have done so if there were not some innate receptivity to the vision. A whole generation was born with Pluto conjuncting Neptune, including the German Jews who were victimised and the Allied armies who fought Germany and Italy and Japan. The eruption of the collective vision of this generation belonged as much to the "good" side as the "bad," just as the same experience binds the rapist and the raped, or the murderer and the murdered.

One may well ask why what erupted was so particularly odious. I don't think this odiousness is inherent in the conjunction, although one would expect Pluto and Neptune to produce something drastic and obsessive for good or ill. But I think if energies like this, which contain both a dark and a light pole, try to surface through a particular kind of cultural lopsidedness or paralysis, then the likelihood is that it is predominantly the dark face which will reveal itself. The same principle I think applies both to an individual and to a nation. If an individual is lopsided and overdeveloped in one direction and frozen and twisted and underdeveloped in another, then the eruption of the unconscious brings up the lopsided shadow with it. I don't feel it's coincidental that both Pluto and Neptune are feminine planets, dealing with the emotional and instinctual and imaginal realms. Germany has always been a peculiarly patriarchal culture, whose chief deity was a male storm-god, Wotan. The development of the feminine side of the psyche in Germany was perhaps rather handicapped by the bias of the cultural values. So when these two

feminine planets burst through, it would seem reasonable to suppose that they would behave in a pretty archaic way when they
did.

You can see that without hindsight one could not determine
that this was Hitler's chart. But you could determine that this is
an individual who has a propensity to be taken over by the collective unconscious. If you bear this in mind, and then consider his
tenth house Saturn in Leo with its suggestion of personal ambition
and almost overwhelming need to compensate for his loneliness
and isolation and repressed anger through public recognition,
then you can see how the two separate things might combine. The
tenth house Saturn also describes the very difficult mother-
relationship he had, with a domineering and overpossessive mother
and a father who died when he was quite young. This kind of
family background and rather neurotic drive are not especially
uncommon. The insecurity and ambition would naturally force
him to seek recognition, and to seek it in a distorted way with
rather grandiose fantasies of his own importance and talent. As
soon as he achieves any position of this kind, then the Pluto-
Neptune drive would begin to push through into the public eye.
You can then put these things together with the Mercury-Uranus
opposition across the ascendant-descendant axis, which suggests
a very fine capacity to grasp the intricacies of an ideology or
political system and articulate it in a Libran, that is, logical and
reasonable, way. I think the key to the whole chart is the unaspected Pluto-Neptune conjunction.

Now, all this hindsight is very nice. But the problem is that
when a conjunction like this is percolating in the collective, an
entire generation is bound to it without being at all aware of what
is happening. The ordinary decent citizen who lives on the surface
of life, be he English, American, German, French, Italian or
whatever, sits around with his rather narrow vision of reality and
then suddenly, the next thing he knows, there is an oppressive
government in power, left or right, and then he shrugs and says,
"Well, I was only following orders. What could I have done? They
would have shot me if I had argued." And he never puts two and
two together, that he and his millions of fellows if they had been
just a little more conscious, would have seen what was happening
in the world outside because they would have seen it in themselves first. This is why I tend to keep going on and on about
what these things represent within the individual, because if there

is a potent outer planet influence in your own horoscope then there is a powerful current at work in your generation group and therefore in you. If you, or I, don't understand what that is about, then someone else will sooner or later announce it, by saying, "I am the voice who can answer all of your aspirations. I am the one who knows better than you what you need." And then you're caught, hypnotised, and you follow, and then you cease to be an individual at all.

Now let's move on to Karl Marx's chart and the Uranus-Neptune conjunction under which he was born. These two planets together suggest a mystical or religious vision coupled with a

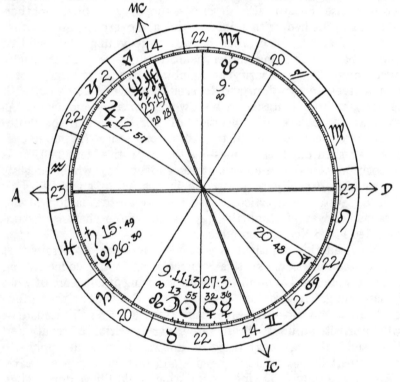

Illustration 3: BIRTH CHART OF KARL MARX
      May 5, 1818, 2:00 AM, Treves, Prussia
   Source: Wemyss, <u>Famous Nativities</u>, "2:00 AM as
   recorded" (Jones, <u>Sabian Symbols</u> gives 1:30 AM).

political ideology. The Plutonian element is absent here in the conjunction, but Saturn and Pluto are in square to it. We can deal with the Uranus-Neptune conjunction first.

This is another individual who was born at a time when the collective was seized with the germ of a new vision. The conjunction falls in Marx's tenth house, which suggests that his calling or vocation would be intimately connected to giving that vision form in society. In Hitler's chart, the outer planet conjunction falls in a watery house, the eighth. It's lurking in the unconscious. Hitler wasn't "called" in the sense of a vocation. He was called to aggrandise himself personally, and became a victim of this unconscious conjunction. But with Marx you might say that he felt personally impelled to contribute this philosophy, even though it isn't really "his." The politico-religious vision of Uranus-Neptune is really Marx's profession. I find it interesting that it's pitted against Saturn and Pluto in the first house of the chart. Although Saturn and Pluto are not technically in conjunction, both are in square to the Uranus-Neptune conjunction. Now I mentioned before that neither Saturn nor Pluto are especially fond of authority, because both of these planets try to claim authority for themselves. On a personal level, Marx was an autocrat, he had a terrifically domineering personality. But his political philosophy is completely different, and the man is at odds with what he preaches. There is a terrific conflict within this chart, between the autocrat and the humanitarian. In Hitler's chart there isn't really a conflict. He was just rolled along by the power of the Pluto-Neptune conjunction. But I think that Marx probably suffered from this conflict between his principles and his personality. Here is someone who believes in freedom yet is personally autocratic. I think also that Marxism contains a kind of projection of one end of this conflict. The tyrannical, controlling enemy is found without rather than within. These squares between Saturn and Pluto and the Uranus-Neptune conjunction are very difficult, and it isn't surprising that even a man of Marx's intellectual stature couldn't cope with the ambivalence of being both a dictator and a member of the ordinary mass. The fantasy of a perfect state which is like a benign mother-god, taking care of each individual and free of greed and aggression, is I think very much the kind of image I would associate with Uranus-Neptune, especially as this conjunction falls in Sagittarius which is prone to be terribly idealistic anyway. But Saturn in the first house will always seek to protect its own territory first, because it's much too cynical to believe that people can will themselves into altruism because of a theory. And Pluto of course obeys jungle law, because it's also too realistic about the darker aspects of human nature to trust in anyone doing something just because it might help humanity.

I find this chart very interesting, because you cannot separate a philosophy or a psychological system from the person who propounds it. I am also very interested in the way in which Marxism is interpreted. Whatever Marx meant by his vision, it has certainly taken on some strange forms in the twentieth century. Most Marxists that I have met are very annoyed if I suggest that their political system is really a religious vision, because the Marxist is supposed to be militantly atheistic. But militant atheism is, in American jargon, a dead giveaway, because if a person is really an atheist he simply doesn't care. If he's militant, he's trying to stamp out something in himself.

I would like you now to look at Lenin's chart which I have put up on the board, because it's quite fascinating to see the way in which Lenin interpreted Marx. Are there any questions or comments first about these two charts?

Audience: Both Hitler and Marx have the sun in Taurus. Can you comment on that?

Liz: Only the usual, which is to describe the basic characteristics of Taurus which you all know. The sun describes what a person is really like, what kinds of things he personally values and wants to express in his life. In Hitler's case I fear it was mainly the more negative aspects of Taurus that showed themselves, because there was so little room for a healthy personality to express itself. Taurus is a deeply sensual and physical sign, and the squares of Venus and Mars to Saturn suggest that any opportunity of living this sensual nature in a harmonious way was blocked by fear and isolation and mistrust. I think that if you frustrate something so basic, it turns cruel. I have seen this before with both Taurus and Scorpio, because both signs are so instinctual and cannot really reflect reasonably on the causes of their frustration without considerable effort. So they turn vicious out of hurt and rage. If you frustrate the sensuality that is inherent in Taurus, it can turn brutal. But I don't really think the historical Hitler that we see in film clips has any Taurus left to show. There's nothing but Pluto-Neptune pouring out.

Audience: It's interesting that Hitler had a knowledge and interest in astrology. I wonder to what extent he manipulated that knowledge to support his political ideas.

Liz: To a great extent. It's pretty common knowledge now that Hitler had a stable full of astrologers to advise him, and when they began to advise him with warnings instead of promises of victory he began to shoot them. It's a risky profession. There was an immense revival of magical cults during Hitler's rule, and military orders like the SS were quite heavily steeped in ritual magic. There is quite a lot of interesting literature available on the influence of occult societies before and during the Third Reich. I suppose these too were part of the Pluto-Neptune vision to which he was sensitive. He certainly manipulated all of it. Even the silver and black that dominate the visual presentation of the Reich are symbolic, ceremonial colours, and the swastika is an ancient symbol. There was a very extensive knowledge of the use of such things in Hitler's party. It's certainly very Plutonian, because it plays on the unconscious of the nation.

Both these charts show the potential for a certain kind of personality with certain kinds of motivations. The missing piece to the mystery of why people like Marx and Hitler affect the world so profoundly lies, I think, in the world, rather than in the horoscopes. If the collective needs a particular kind of mouthpiece for its inarticulate longings and needs, then it will find one. Marx seems to have been more of a Taurus than Hitler because he managed to live a stable family life in a rather traditional way. But no one would have paid any attention to *Das Kapital* if it had not embodied something that answered a secret collective longing for a large group of people. Both these charts show a propensity to serve as a mouthpiece for a particular collective vision. You can't look at Hitler's chart without hindsight and say, "This man is going to be responsible for the murder of six million Jews and the destruction of half of Europe." If it were ever possible to work out the chart of Jesus Christ, and there have certainly been speculations enough, I am sure we would be completely baffled at the absence of anything superhuman. But the longing for a Messiah was hot to boiling at the time of Christ's birth, and the man and the myth ran together. I doubt that you would find a configuration in the chart which said, "This is the Messiah." The same ten planets were in the heavens then as are in the heavens now. But the dawn of the Piscean Age had arrived, and the collective needed

a new myth and a new vision of God. This is why I am so interested in what happens to individuals where the outer planets are
strongly marked in the horoscope. They are prone to becoming
vessels for the collective, but if they live this out unwittingly and
unconsciously, then they may become victims of the collective,
or express its longings in a rather unpleasant way.

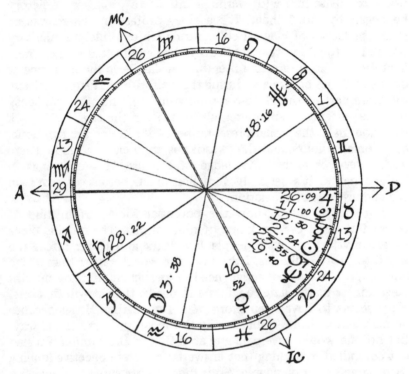

Illustration 4: BIRTH CHART OF NIKOLAI LENIN
April 22, 1870 (NS), 9:42 PM, Ulyanousk, Russia
Source: Erlewine, Circle Book of Charts, who gives
        his source as Rudhyar, American Astrology
        magazine, June 1938.

Now let's look at Lenin's chart. Remember that in Marx's
horoscope Uranus and Neptune are conjuncting. Here in Lenin's
chart, Neptune is in 19 degrees of Aries, in square to Uranus in
18 degrees of Cancer. The conjunction for which Marx was a
mouthpiece has here appeared as a square, which I think is very

relevant in terms of the way Lenin interpreted Marx. The politico-religious vision in Marx is a unity, it's all of a piece and has the powerful suggestion of an answer. In Lenin the vision splinters, and one half is opposed to the other. Here is another first house Saturn, which is interesting. It seems that both these men who professed to have such concern for the rights and freedoms of others were not actually very prone to offering it in actual life. And we have another sun in Taurus here. Although Marx thought religion was the opiate of the masses, his vision was permeated with a kind of religious idealism, a feeling for the brotherhood of man which comes from a heart level as much as an intellectual one. In Lenin, there does not seem to have been any possibility of bringing together the feeling values of Neptune with the hard political system of Uranus.

The way in which we tend to experience squares is that two urges or needs or sets of values are fighting. This is a very basic interpretive principle. The combination of energies, Uranus and Neptune, is the same whether it's a square or a conjunction. There is an attempt to bring together the theoretical evolutionary vision of Uranus with the mystical longings of Neptune. But the difference between the conjunction and the square lies in the way the individual experiences them. If they are in conjunction, they feel like something united, that can potentially be put together. If they are in square, they feel like two irreconcilably conflicting things, and the person will generally take the side of one against the other. I think that the militant atheism which I mentioned before is typical of the square rather than the conjunction. The square makes it an obsessive issue. If you side with Uranus against Neptune, which would be more likely in Lenin's case because his moon is in Aquarius and his sun in Taurus and he would be inclined more to the rational thinking side of things, then it seems that mysticism is going to be the enemy of the ideological system. Not only mysticism, but everything Neptunian, which means the arts and the imagination in general. Lenin's idea of communism has a very different flavour from that of Marx, because he has made Neptune the enemy.

Uranus and Neptune were in opposition just before and during the First World War, during the period leading up to the Russian Revolution and the seizing of power by the Bolsheviks. This is an interesting aspect which will probably appear in the charts of some of the older members of the group. The opposition started with

Uranus in Capricorn opposing Neptune in Cancer, and continued for a while into Aquarius and Leo. I have done quite a number of charts for people belonging to this group, and one of the things that has struck me, which I hope does not upset anyone here, is that this is a sacrificial generation. It has passed through two world wars, terrible economic depression, and the complete destruction and transformation of social and personal values. Neptune in Cancer is intensely mystical and devotional, not just about God but also about the home, the family, the fatherland or motherland, the parents, and the little plot of land one owns. Wherever Neptune is, that is where a generation tries to experience the divine. Cancerian things become sacred to the group with Neptune in Cancer. This is pitted against the hard reality of Uranus in Capricorn, where the world is an impersonal place which can only be made sane and orderly by discipline, hard work, and obedience to temporal law. The economic and political horrors that this generation has passed through seem to me to reflect the split between one set of values and another.

In a sense, these three examples of the aspect reflect three different renditions of the same thing. Marx gives voice to the conjunction as a vision of human potential. Lenin comes along and gives voice to the same vision, but it has fallen apart and now seems only possible if some fundamental feeling values are stamped out. Soviet Russia and a whole generation of people born at the same time experience this vision as an impossible tension between opposites, first trying to go one way and then another. The sentimental vision of human brotherhood and the cold cynicism of an order which requires rigid authority to keep coherence are now completely at odds. Uranus and Neptune will be conjuncting again in the 1990's. Perhaps there is a chance for that generation to bring the whole thing back together again.

Audience: It seems as if it isn't possible to have an objective vision of things without getting your own chart mixed up in it.

Liz: Yes, of course. How are we supposed to see except through our own eyes? You can't separate a person from his politics or his philosophy or his beliefs. There always have been and always will be people who propound theories of human nature and social development, believing that they have discovered the truth. What they have discovered is their truth. This applies to psychologists such as Freud and Jung as well. It applies on every level, to all the different branches and schools of therapy and education. One can only describe one's own experience of life, even if it is a collective vision which also belongs to a generation of people. Even if your theory is based on observation, the observer affects his experiment and selects those "facts" which reflect what he perceives as facts. There is no such thing as an objective psychology, unless this is taken into account. Jung began his work as a disciple of Freud. Then he broke away, because he disagreed with certain fundamental concepts in Freud's system and his experience showed him other things. But what his experience showed him was his experience, which was in turn coloured by his own psyche and his own horoscope. Perhaps he saw more than Freud. Naturally my personal feeling is that he did. But that was contingent on his own perceptions being potentially broader. And he certainly didn't see everything.

Let's have a look at the charts of Freud and Jung. Freud was a Taurus with Scorpio rising. Although Freud, like Marx, decried religion, God was alive and well and hiding in the sexual instinct. For Jung, who was unashamedly religious although in a rather unorthodox way, God was alive and well and hiding in the core of human individuality. That is not surprising in light of his sun in Leo and his Aquarian ascendant. If you consider the psychological viewpoints of these two great men in terms of their horoscopes, it becomes apparent that they have each focussed on what they understand best. Where they differ from Joe Bloggs who runs the Psychocybernetic-Gestalt-Massage Centre down the street and who also has a map of the human psyche, is a bit of a mystery, because I don't think horoscopes show genius. But both Freud and Jung have the sun in strong aspect to an outer planet, which at least suggests that they were receptive to a more transpersonal or deeper level of human experience than just their own personal lives. They are not only describing their own psychologies, but also something broader, more collective, more universal.

Freud had the sun conjuncting Uranus. In a sense Freudian psychology is a kind of ideology, a map of social restructuring, because the rampaging *id* which is the source of human pathology must be first understood and then tamed by the ego. Freedom from the imprisoning terrors of the unconscious comes from understanding and harnessing the natural forces. This is very Uranian. Freud wanted very badly to be scientific, and on the

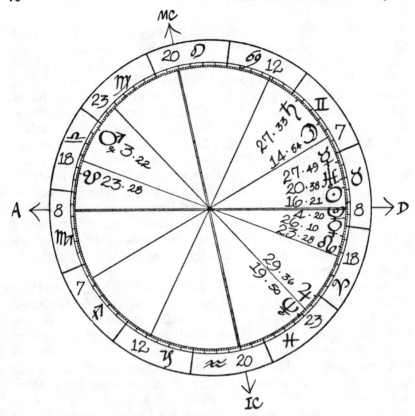

Illustration 5: BIRTH CHART OF SIGMUND FREUD
May 6, 1856, 6:30 PM, Freiburg, Germany
Source: Jones, The Life & Work of Sigmund Freud

surface he seems to be, although underneath you can feel the
dogmatism and rigidity which are not really part of a truly scientific viewpoint. But Freud had absolutely no time for the mystical.
Human biology was a great mystery for him, but he persisted in
seeing it as nature rather than as nature and spirit both. Jung also
tried to present himself scientifically, but it comes across as
more of a surface irritation, an annoyance with his psychiatric
colleagues that he has not been taken seriously. But it is obviously
an imaginal and nonrational experience that drives him, rather
than an ideology. He had the sun in exact square to Neptune.
Religious feeling is apparent throughout his work, and the road to

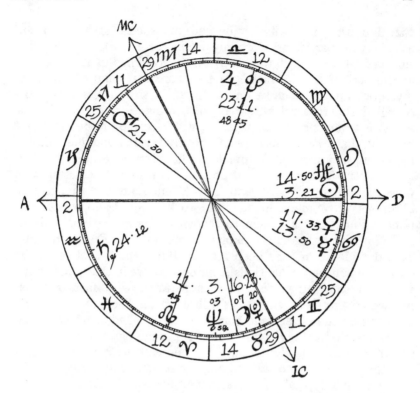

Illustration 6: BIRTH CHART OF CARL GUSTAV JUNG
July 26, 1875, 7:32 PM, Kesswil, Switzerland
Source: Baumann-Jung, "Some Reflections on the
Horoscope of C.G. Jung," Spring, 1975.

an experience of the numinous is through submission to it, rather than control of it. That is very Neptunian.

Both these men had the sun placed in the seventh house. They would therefore be likely to develop their own individualities through the catalyst of others, which is of course the core of all analytic work. Whether an analyst is Freudian or Jungian, it is the relationship between two people which is the cornerstone of the work. They both gave expression to the outer planet vision through vocations which involved others.

Audience: What was Freud's attitude toward astrology?

Liz: I don't know whether he had any special attitude toward astrology in particular. Certainly in his early work anything that smacked of the occult was an irritation to him. But it seems that at the end of his life he began to reconsider some of the more mysterious phenomena he encountered. It isn't surprising that the so-called supernatural would be disturbing to a sun in Taurus, which is a very pragmatic sign. But with Scorpio on the ascendant he can't have been unaware of the mysterious and inexplicable happenings in a person's life. I would interpret a great conflict between the Taurean scientist and the Scorpionic fascination with mysterious depths. One cannot avoid encountering strange synchronous phenomena in analytic work. Any dealings with the unconscious force a person to recognise the nonrational side of life. Not everything can be explained biologically. Freud's Scorpio ascendant led him very deep indeed. But I think that of all the signs, the sun in Taurus finds it hardest to live in that nonrational world. If something can't be demonstrated with facts and explained concretely, then Taurus will recoil and become frightened.

Jung on the other hand wasn't at all impelled to reject the so-called occult world. He postulated it psychologically rather than esoterically, but he didn't have to repudiate it. From very early life he was subject to strange inner experiences and visions. This seems to me typical of the sun-Neptune aspect. Also, as a fire sign, he had less need to relate everything to the body. One can see this difference among many astrologers. Uranus is supposed to rule astrology, but I think that many more Uranian astrologers are really interested in the system and the laws which lie behind the system. The logical basis of astrology appeals to Uranus. So does the research side of it. The magical element is rather offensive to Uranus, in the sense of something inexplicable which must be felt rather than understood. The Neptunian viewpoint is more comfortable with the subjective experience of astrology, and the imagery of it, and the more so-called spiritual aspect of it. Someone who is terribly Neptunian will often find statistical research quite offensive, because it denies any kind of fluidity or subjective reality. Jung was of course not wholly Neptunian, because of his Aquarian ascendant and Saturn rising in Aquarius. I think he suffered a conflict between the richness of his inner experiences and perceptions and the need to communicate them in a logical way which would be comprehensible to his colleagues. But I think at the core, the bias of Jung's work is toward Neptune, while the bias of Freud's is toward Uranus. And the strange paradox is that it is Freud's work which comes across with a more dogmatic religious tone, while Jung's is much more open and reasonable.

Audience: Are you saying that the two points of view are completely incompatible?

Liz: No, I'm not saying that at all. But I think it's difficult to find the place where they meet. The experience of Neptune's world defies the intellect. It's terribly difficult to communicate, let alone justify with any kind of logical system. But a purely Neptunian mysticism without any grounding in the laws of reality is worse than useless, because it can delude the person into believing that his vision is greater than reality. One without the other is incomplete. I think we need both points of view. But they are hard to put together, because we tend to favour one or the other. It seems that this kind of pairing of opposites is a basic propensity in human beings. The conscious attitude takes one side and the unconscious takes the other and starts tugging. When a person tries terribly hard to explain everything from a rational basis, that is when he is in most danger of becoming irrational in his obsession with rationality. The moment he tries to dissociate himself from the evidence of his senses and the facts of the world around him, that is when he is in most danger of becoming hyper-rational in his attempts to control his reality. Neitzche wrote about the opposing viewpoints of the Apollonian and the Dionysian, which have a tendency to switch places if they are pushed too far.

This is largely why I am a little cynical about ideologies and polarised political viewpoints. The further you take the right or the left, the more they become like each other. They become each other. Hitler and Stalin are interchangeable. I think a good example of this is the tract that was published in *The Humanist* a while ago by a number of scientists against astrology. Probably most of you have seen it or heard of it. It was an attempt to debunk astrology in the name of science. It was so emotional and irrational that it made me fall about laughing, although it was attempting to say that those who believe in astrology are emotional and irrational people. But this is very common. I think the only place of sanity is somewhere in the middle, giving respect to both worlds.

Audience: Is it likely that people who have contacts between an inner planet and both Uranus and Neptune are going to feel compelled to choose between them?

Liz: Yes, I think this is what happened to Lenin. Uranus and Neptune are in square, and with a square the tendency is to side with one end and project the other one. The rejected end of the square becomes the enemy outside. I think something similar would have happened if he had had the sun conjuncting one and square the other. It's very useful, if you have these strong outer planet contacts in the chart, especially if two contradictory ones such as Uranus and Neptune are involved, to consider what sort of ideologies or collectives you like and dislike intensely. It's an excellent exercise. Do you despise socialism? Do you loathe capitalism? Do you hate wealthy businessmen? Do you idealise the unions? Do you have a horror of religious people? Do you think the peace movement can do no wrong, or the police no right? It's very revealing to reflect on one's strong collective antagonisms and idealisations. You'll often find outer planets involved in squares and oppositions to inner ones with very strong or obsessive likes and dislikes in this kind of direction. Very often Saturn gets cast as the arch-conservative, and Pluto as the fascist. Uranus will wear the face of the revolutionary, and Neptune the peace-loving utopian dreamer.

I have noticed a typical pattern with Pluto squares and oppositions to the sun. These people often complain of others who come into their lives and dominate or manipulate them. They are often very liberal themselves, and have a horror or a loathing of anything powerful or ruthless. Yet they are carrying this propensity in themselves. I was very interested in the way in which Jimmy Carter, who has a sun-Pluto square, got himself tangled up with a dictator like Khomeini. In some way there was a strange fate about that collision. My fantasy is that Khomeini acted out Carter's Pluto. Carter was the reasonable Libran trying to be fair and co-operative. His own unlived strength and ruthlessness materialised for him in the world.*

---

*Another good example more recently is Mrs. Thatcher, who is also a Libran with sun in square to Pluto, and whose entanglement with the Argentinian *junta* has a similar fatedness about it.

Audience: Can you talk about the Uranus-Pluto conjunction in Virgo?

Liz: Yes, certainly. That conjunction was operative from around 1963 through to 1968. For a period of time during those five years, between the spring of 1964 through the end of 1966, Saturn was hovering around in opposition to the conjunction. Uranus together with Pluto suggests to me a political vision coupled with an urgent need to destroy old forms and attitudes. It's obviously rather obsessive and potentially violent. The keynote with Neptune, which if you remember was coupled with Pluto in Hitler's chart, is salvation for divine ends. But the keynote with Uranus is freedom from constraint, and if you put this with Pluto's urgent emotional necessity, then the seeking of that freedom isn't likely to be particularly gentle.

I am better versed with what was happening in America during that time than I am with what was happening in Great Britain because I was living in America then. Of course my perceptions and memories are subjective ones, but they might point in a particular direction. One of the major events that occurred under the conjunction was the Viet Nam War. I don't think the war itself is necessarily typical of the conjunction, since we tend to have wars going on all the time and just about any heavy configuration appears to set them off. But the repercussions of that war are very important. There was a tremendous rebellion against it, of a unique kind. I think the general attitude in the two World Wars was that it was noble to fight for your country because that was what you were brought up to believe. If you were conscripted, then you went to war, and you didn't question the rightness of it. But people didn't react in that way to Viet Nam. The unquestioned acceptance of authority broke down. The sixties of course saw the birth of the drug and dropout generation, the great hippie movement. The things which were being attacked were typically Virgoan: ordinary nine-to-five jobs, humdrum worldly existence, unquestioned obedience to the system, petty materialism, preoccupation with order and conventional morality.

The vision of a freer and more meaningful life was not pursued with care and forethought, of course, because Pluto isn't interested in preserving what is of value in the old order. It just wants to wipe the slate clean. That is what a great many people did during the sixties. Now the generation of people who were born then are now in their 'teens. I don't think it's a generalisation to say that they are a very intense and anarchistic group in many ways. Their music reflects the inherent violence of Uranus-Pluto. It's quite different from the rock music which emerged from the people born with Uranus in Gemini in trine to Neptune in Libra. Punk rock is violent and nihilistic. It's a bit different from Woodstock. There is quite a lot of violence coming from this group in Great Britain at the moment. They are embodying the same strange spirit that passed through those of us who are older during the sixties. Perhaps when they begin to reach mid-life and the age of greatest external effectiveness, they will truly change the old order. I would expect the thrust of this to be in the areas of work, health, ecology, all the typical Virgo areas.

Some of this group have Saturn in opposition to the Uranus-Pluto conjunction. Saturn has been moving through Virgo lately, and I think this may have some connection with the violence that is erupting, because Saturn always tries to actualise things. Saturn has been triggering that conjunction. Who can blame them for being violent? That combination of planets is terribly explosive, and a fifteen- or sixteen-year-old psyche cannot contain it as constructively as a forty-year-old.

Audience: It would be very interesting to meet a cross-section of the young people born during the Uranus-Pluto conjunction who are the children of the hippie generation, just to see the difference in consciousness.

Liz: I have met two or three. That doesn't count as a statistic. But those two or three charts that I've done have suggested certain things to me. The parents all have Uranus in Gemini and Neptune in Libra, and often they are in trine. There is a typically airy idealism about this group. Even the people born with Saturn conjunct Uranus in Taurus have the conjunction in trine to Neptune. The vision of a new world is very strong, but it's a vision that comes out through ideas, music, attitudes about love and personal relationships, things that are much gentler. Their children are more cynical, just as the hippie generation rebelled against cynical parents. Here the offspring are the cynical ones. The earthy sign in which the conjunction falls comes through very strongly. We usually imagine that the parents, who are older and have experienced more, are therefore more realistic and worldly. But here it seems to be reversed. These children are very bitter and very pragmatic. Perhaps they need to be. I don't really know.

When major transits occur over one of these outer planet configurations, it's like a signal which mobilises an entire generation. It's almost a sort of massive army, a group which has an undeclared purpose in terms of collective evolution and development, and when the natal configuration is triggered, then the army is sent into action. Obviously these things occur in the unconscious. But I think it's this effect of transits later on over the natal configurations of outer planets which bring the meaning of the thing out into society. You might notice that all your friends of the same age group begin going through personal crises at the same time. The group is like an organism, and begins moving through important stages of development, although if you see this individual by individual you might not make the connection. Of course there are casualties when these triggers occur. Some people can't meet the challenge, or the pressure on the psyche becomes too great. Others strengthen and become very creative. I am convinced that generations have a meaning and a purpose just as an individual has a meaning and a purpose for being alive, although it's perhaps impossible to ever really know fully in a rational way what that meaning might be.

I mentioned the group born with Uranus in opposition to Neptune in the first decades of the century. Perhaps these people were meant in some way to be a sacrificial group. They certainly suffered a great many things which we will very likely never suffer, as though they cleaned something out of the collective for those of us who came later. That is perhaps a rather mystical way of looking at it, but I sometimes have the feeling that these people are a kind of bridge over which their children and grandchildren have walked. Some of them are very sorry for themselves, and therefore antagonistic toward younger people who do not have to suffer what they suffered. But many others I have met seem to have an understanding of this contribution to the next generation through sacrifice and the taking on of a burden. There is a synchronicity between outer worldly events and the individuals who grow up through those events. The people produce the events and are also the recipients of them. In some way they are the same thing.

Perhaps people who are not bound by strong outer planet

configurations are in some way freer. I'm sure that to have Uranus conjunct Pluto in your birth chart means that you are driven toward some collective end, and your personal life is going to be affected by that in a way which other people are not. Some generations are terribly strongly marked, and obviously stand for something, while others are more blurred and are simply people moving through life. If you are tied by the outer planets, then you as an individual are tied to the collective in some unusual way. And if this is so, then I suspect it's very wise to get some sense of what that might mean. Your fate is bound up with the collective, and it may become very difficult to pursue a life of benign placid continuity, either because you yourself suffer from an intense inner restlessness, or because the world rather nastily intrudes on you. But in the end the inner and the outer correspond, and we all meet the outer planets in one place or the other, if not both.

Lecture Four

Before we begin today, are there any leftover questions from the last session?

Audience: When you're talking about generation influences, the influences of the outer planets, do you use larger orbs than those you would use for a natal chart?

Liz: No, I would use the same orbs, of around eight to ten degrees for conjunctions and squares and oppositions. But I think that two planets in the same sign, even if they are not technically conjuncting, tend to give some feeling of a conjunction. That is no different from the same thing in a natal chart. For example, during the two years or so that Saturn takes to move through a sign, there will be times when it isn't quite in conjunction with an outer planet also passing through that sign. The two both retrograde and do a little dance back and forth together. I think there is some of the same feeling during those gaps, but it isn't quite as intense an influence. A person with an exact or close conjunction will naturally feel the impact much more powerfully.

Audience: You would use an orb as wide as ten degrees?

Liz: Yes, particularly with a conjunction. There seems to be a lot of argument about orbs, and I can only tell you what I have learned to use from my own experience. I'm inclined to give importance to wide aspects, but I would look quite carefully at which planets were involved. I would certainly use ten degrees for major aspects involving the sun, moon and Saturn. I also think it depends on where these planets are placed, so that if the sun is, say, in the midheaven, it will be very prominent in the chart, and then I would consider that its sphere of influence is greater. I also suspect that it depends on the person. A very loose conjunction or square will give the same characteristics as a tight one, but they are more diluted, and the individual has more flexibility with it. Also, if he's putting a lot of energy into working at that aspect, or developing it in his life, then it will become more obvious because it's becoming more conscious.

An example of this might be a person with a wide sun-Neptune trine or conjunction who decides to study music. Although the looseness of the aspect means there isn't the same compulsive feeling, the fact that he's trying to develop himself along the lines of the aspect means that it will become more important in his life. I know that a good many astrologers like using narrow orbs of six to eight degrees, but that is simply how I feel about it.

This same problem of orbs arises when you're trying to interpret transits and progressions as well. Many people think of transits and progressions as operative only when they are exact. But I feel there is a period of build-up which goes on for quite a long time before the aspect is exact. You can smell it in the wind, so to speak, before it becomes apparent in your life. With a major progression such as that of the sun over a natal planet, I think there is a three or four year build-up. It doesn't just suddenly arrive one morning out of nowhere. The psyche has been preparing for it for some time. I feel we are sometimes a little too tight and literal in the way we work with orbs.

I would like to talk now about the signs which the outer planets rule, because there are colourations in these signs which I think are not terribly easy to understand if you are considering them from the old traditional descriptions. Our understanding of the three outer planets is very new, and there is no reason to suppose that our understanding of Scorpio, Aquarius and Pisces is all that complete. These signs are all co-ruled, as you know. Scorpio used to be assigned to Mars, Aquarius to Saturn and Pisces to Jupiter. Scorpio was called the night house of Mars in medieval astrology, Aquarius was the day house of Saturn and Pisces was the night house of Jupiter. The two signs given to Saturn, Capricorn and Aquarius, were said to reflect two different faces of Saturn. One represented the principle of order and boundaries expressing itself on the material plane, and the other the same principle on the mental or spiritual plane. Pisces and Sagittarius were said to reflect the principle of expansion and growth and faith on the emotional plane and the intellectual one respectively. And Aries and Scorpio were said to represent the principle of aggression and will operating on the creative and procreative levels. So our old descriptions of Aries and Scorpio describe both as willful and determined, but Aries becomes the pioneer or the athlete, while Scorpio becomes the disciplined soldier or surgeon. Pisces becomes the priest or the nurse, while Sagittarius becomes the philosopher or teacher. Capricorn becomes the businessman or the politician, while Aquarius becomes the scientist or social reformer. I think you are all familiar with these traditional readings of the signs. You can still find them in modern textbooks, and I think they are true so far as they go. It's a great mistake to dispense with the old rulers. I am certain that they are still valid, and one of the ways in which this can be seen is when Mars makes a major progression and you see the repercussions through the house which Scorpio rules in the birth chart.

For example, the Saturnian element is very obvious in Aquarius. If you get into an ideological discussion, you become aware of the orderliness and discipline of Aquarius' thinking, and even sometimes of the rigidity and conservatism, although the ideas themselves may be eclectic and innovative. The competitive instinct in Scorpio is very obvious as well. Scorpio is just as determined to win as Aries, but he just tends to be quieter about it. And the religious feeling and hopefulness which is associated with Sagittarius is just as apparent in Pisces.

But despite the importance of the old rulers, I think that these three signs need to be involved in some way with the collective. Because of the connection with the outer planets, they are bound to issues larger than the personal. I have seen a very sad and lost look many times in Scorpios and Aquarians and Pisceans when their lives are too narrow and dedicated wholly to personal pursuits. I feel this is because something in these signs needs a link with larger human movements and endeavours. If you take the typical Aquarian or Piscean and put him to work in a bank and give him no outlets, not even reading, where he can swim in wider waters, then I think he becomes increasingly frustrated and restless and neurotic, because the nature of the signs requires some kind of deeper food. We are all familiar with cases where the sun in any sign can become frustrated and twisted because of difficult aspects to it, or because the individual can't live his own nature out in context of his environment and his lifestyle. Earlier I mentioned Hitler as a rather twisted sun in Taurus. I think the same applies to Scorpio, Pisces and Aquarius, but the real nature of these signs is a little less simple, and the average collective blueprint for life doesn't take into account those broader needs.

When I am talking about these three signs, I hope you realise that I don't mean only the sun placed there, but also the ascendant and any other emphasis such as a stellium. The same principle

applies. But because the sun is so bound up with personal fulfillment and confidence, it's much more obvious if the person's life
doesn't mirror his own internal needs. By the way, I also hope you
realise that when I say "collective" I don't mean "spiritual." I
am not equating these terms in any way. When Jung writes about
the collective unconscious, he is not implying that it is a higher
spiritual entity. The eruption of Nazi Germany should be a good
illustration. Jung referred to the collective as the "objective
psyche," by which he meant that it was much older and deeper
and more inclusive than the individual's personal, subjective
psychic experience. It contains the heritage of the whole of man's
development as well as man's future, but no one person can
encompass it, hence it is "objective." Strong outer planet contacts
don't make you "spiritual," whatever that means, nor are they
"more evolved." There are few less evolved spiritual beings than
some of the masterpieces of brutality whose charts we have looked
at such as Hitler and Lenin, so lest you imagine that prominent
outer planets confer God's grace, remember them along with any
number of people locked up in psychiatric hospitals. I once met a
rather peculiar lady who said she was an "esoteric astrologer," and
she told me that only people with the sun in aspect to Neptune
were capable of spiritual evolvement. I am afraid I think this is
rather idiotic, since I once did the chart of a pedigreed poodle who
had the sun in aspect to Neptune, and he was a very obnoxious
dog.

I hope I have made this clear. Perhaps I should have said it
earlier, since there is a good deal of pseudo-spirituality around
among astrologers. Strong aspects to the outer planets mean, I
feel, that your life will be connected to a greater or lesser extent
with the larger collective movements and yearnings of your time.
How this manifests depends very much on your time, as well as
your own capacity to give shape to these things. At any rate, I
feel there is a necessity in Scorpio, Aquarius and Pisces to find
someplace in their lives for a view of reality that extends beyond
the purely personal sphere. Otherwise I think these signs can
become terribly negative. They have the worst reputations of all
the zodiac. The classic charge against Pisces is that of drugs and
alcohol, and so far as I have seen, this is perfectly true. A great
many Pisceans drown in that water, not because the sign is innately alcoholic, but because they are thirsting for something
beyond a wholly material perception of reality. The opening of

the door might come through a strong religious aspiration, or a creative outlet such as music or poetry or acting, or an experience of the unity of life that comes through service of some kind. But if the door is never opened, then the only way to the spirit is through spirits, if you will excuse the horrible pun. I think this is very important to consider if you are doing vocational counseling, for obvious reasons. Even if Pisces wants to go and study computers or become a civil servant, he must still have some place in his life for the myths and the music and the poetry and the imagination.

There are a good many pathetic Pisceans wandering about trying desperately to become good accountants or stock brokers or insurance agents and wondering why they feel so hopeless and depressed and lethargic while their Taurean and Capricornian compatriots really enjoy their jobs. The same problem applies with Scorpio. I think that Scorpio is very bound up with the darkness of the collective, and with the primitive and primordial instincts that have been repressed and shut out by civilised society. Scorpio needs to be connected with this great reservoir of dark vital life. If he isn't involved with it, either through psychology or medicine or politics or whatever, then I think it turns poisonous in him and bursts out toward other people or becomes self-destructive. If he tries to pretend that such things don't exist, then they come at him from the outside. And I think Aquarius must be involved with the idea of progress, the idea of the possibilities of man in some way. He needs to know that he is part of a larger human family that is moving somewhere, toward something. Otherwise he begins to become very cranky and obsessive and dissociated.

I wanted to mention this because I feel these three signs are rather eccentric. I hope I haven't insulted anyone. But having an outer planet as a co-ruler complicates things as you can see. We are all collective creatures at bottom, and we are all mouthpieces for whatever is going on in the human family while we are alive. But the focus for some is more diffuse than for others. These three signs are often accused of antisocial behaviour, because they tend toward strange interests and odd viewpoints. I feel that this is natural, due to the rulership of the outer planets. Most of our inbred models of normality are Saturnian, and it is terribly easy for the Piscean and the Scorpio and the Aquarian to feel very misunderstood and peculiar, an outsider.

I think we must also consider the houses of which the three

outer planets are the natural rulers, because I think planets placed in the eighth, eleventh and twelfth can be very troublesome if there is no understanding of them. The traditional meanings given for these houses are pretty thin and unsatisfying. I know that this is familiar material for most of you, but it is worth mentioning. Somehow I am not very edified by finding the eleventh house described as "clubs and societies," or the eighth as either "death" or "legacies." And the twelfth has deeper levels than "hospitals and prisons."

Let's begin with the eighth house. The signs and houses form a cycle of development, a circle of experience that ends with a new beginning. The definitions traditionally given for the first seven houses are usually pretty clear and workable, because up to that point the cycle of development concerns the individual himself, with his own values, attitudes, family, pleasures, habits, and so on. A person is born at the ascendant, and the first house is his identity. Then he begins to develop his resources in the second house, and learns to interact with the environment in the third. He becomes aware of his roots and his need of others in the fourth, and finds his capacity to create in the fifth. In the sixth he refines and perfects the skills of living, and in the seventh he becomes aware of others as objective outer things that are separate from him and must be accommodated.

Then we come to the eighth house. How do we get from the encounter with the other to insurance policies and legacies? I think we must stay with the idea of a cycle. Something happens as a result of an individual's encounter with other people. He will not be the same any more if this encounter has been genuine, because another person will always force you to discover things about yourself you didn't know before. You find that there are undercurrents, drives, even a fate which is at work in any deep relationship, which reveals an entire unseen and unknown world. This is the unconscious, which has a good deal more to say about why we are in relationships than the ego does. So the encounter with the other person in the seventh house leads to the encounter with the other in oneself in the eighth. And the frightening thing about that other is that it is not just one's own. It's all the silt and accummulation of mother and father and masculine and feminine going back for aeons. It's the underworld of the psyche, which is the place to which Persephone gets abducted when Hades or Pluto grabs her and takes her in his black chariot into the halls of the dead. All of Libra's ideas about human interchange tend to fall to pieces when confronted with the Scorpionic side of life, which I think is nicely described by Freud in his work. The eighth house is a battleground, a place of collision. The individual must submit to something other, whether that other is his own repressed darkness or his fate.

Out of this collision there comes the realisation that something other than the ego runs the show. Eventually the other is formulated into a sense of meaning and of the divine, so we move to the ninth house with its quest for the experience of God. If a person encounters fate, he begins to ask questions. From the formulation of a personal philosophy, the individual moves into the tenth house, and tries to actualise his beliefs through some constructive contribution to the world around him. After he has climbed his way up into the world and assumed worldly responsibilities, then he begins to question the point of it all. It begins to dawn on him that he is part of a larger human family with its own vision and pattern of development into the future. He becomes aware that people are not so dissimilar to each other, that the human psyche operates according to certain basic laws and patterns. That is the eleventh house. Finally even the separateness of human individuality fades in the face of the unity of the whole of life, with its past reaching back into the animal and vegetative kingdoms. The matrix or sea of life is there at the bottom, the sea of the unconscious without form or definition. I think the twelfth house is far more than hospitals and confinement. It is the root from which myths spring, the sea of the imagination and the most ancient past.

If you find several planets in the twelfth house in a chart, then I think the individual must learn something about the imaginal realm. If he doesn't come to terms with it then it dismembers him. The twelfth house is a mediumistic house, because it contains the entire history of human experience. This is of course similar to having strong contacts to Neptune, or having a strong emphasis in Pisces. If there are many planets in the eleventh house, then one must learn to work with the movements toward consciousness which are developing during one's lifetime. If there are many planets in the eighth, then the individual must learn to look darkness in the face.

I think that a person can have many problems if the sun or other emphasis highlights one of these three houses, if he tries to approach the crises that life brings him from a very narrow perspective. In some way that individual is living through issues which are critical to the whole group, not just himself. That doesn't mean he shouldn't deal with the personal side of it, but it makes a difference if the broader perspective is understood as well. If you can't see how your own dilemma is in some way exemplary of issues which are critical for your time, then the feelings of isolation and dissociation are often overwhelming.

Audience: What do you think is the difference in meaning between a planet and the house it naturally rules?

Liz: A planet represents a dynamic energy. It's an alive, active thing, which has motives of its own and is trying to get somewhere. A house on the other hand is a realm of experience, a theatre. A planet is an actor, and the house is the backdrop against which the actor plays. If you have the sun conjuncting Neptune, then you have two actors who are wedded to each other, and the two together will represent an urge to transcend life, to touch the divine, to escape the confines of limited material reality. But if you have the sun conjuncting Saturn and they are placed in the twelfth house, the two actors are not concerned with transcendence. They are going to try to build permanence and self-sufficiency and strength to cope with life. But the environment in which they must seek their goal will be the world of dreams, fantasies, inner religious longings, routes for escape back into the original womb. The actors are still going to have to eventually build a strong, solid ego. But their ground of learning will be the mystical world.

The planets in their signs are the stuff of which we're made. The houses are the arenas of life in which we are destined, or fated, to learn to become ourselves. Sometimes these two are horribly opposite, such as Saturn in the twelfth, or Neptune in the second. Sometimes they are in accord, like Jupiter in the ninth or Venus in the seventh. The stuff of which you are made may not agree with the experiences life brings you, but you will be confronted with those experiences over and over again until some kind of fusion or integration begins to happen. I think that in practise the circumstances often sound very similar. But I believe the planets themselves are the most important factors in the chart.

Audience: In your book on Saturn, you use planets and houses as if they were the same thing.

Liz: In practise they sound very similar. It helps us to understand the planet, the sign and the house if we draw comparisons. For example, knowing something about Scorpio's behaviour offers a lot of insight into Pluto, and you need to grasp both to get a sense of the eighth house. The same meaning underlies the trinity of sign, planet, house. But there is a difference, and I think it has to do with motivation versus fate. On some level of course these things are the same. But the planet shows the desire, and the house shows what is permitted. Perhaps it's superfluous to think in terms of separating them, because Venus in the eighth house tells a similar story to Venus in Scorpio and Venus conjunct Pluto. But I find it helpful to differentiate between what is experienced as one's needs and what is experienced as the arena in which those needs are confronted, challenged and met.

Audience: If there are any new planets waiting to be discovered, what will we do with them?

Liz: Assign them as co-rulers, I suppose, in the same way that we have assigned Uranus, Neptune and Pluto. Mercury rules two signs, and perhaps Virgo or Gemini could do with a co-ruler. The same applies to Venus, which rules Taurus and Libra. I'm sure we'd think of something. New planets don't reverse everything we have inherited of traditional astrology. They open up a new dimension both in terms of the meaning of a sign and in terms of human experience. We aren't the same now as we were a century ago, and certainly very different from medieval man. Our consciousness has changed, sometimes for the better and sometimes at great cost. The newly discovered planets reflect newly discovered aspects of life. The three signs co-ruled by the outer planets have a different perceptive orientation from the other nine signs. It's like a kind of developed peripheral vision that picks up things moving in the background that are ordinarily invisible.

Audience: Can you comment on John F. Kennedy's chart? I believe he had a lot of planets in the eighth house.

Liz: Yes, there are five planets in the eighth house. Mars, Mercury

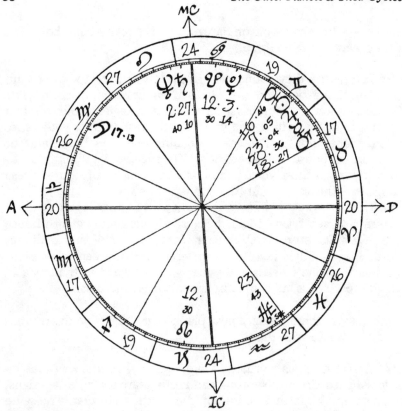

Illustration 7: BIRTH CHART OF JOHN F. KENNEDY
May 29, 1917, 3:15 PM, Brookline, Massachusetts
Source: Doane, <u>Horoscopes of the U.S. Presidents</u>

and Jupiter all conjunct in Taurus, and the sun conjuncts Venus
in Gemini. The Taurus planets are all in square to Uranus in the
fourth house, and the sun-Venus conjunction squares the moon
in Virgo. Apart from what that eighth house emphasis might say
about his sex life, I would interpret it as indicating a man whose
fate would inevitably involve him with the collective shadow.
There is all sorts of behind-the-scenes murk suggested by that
line-up. Saturn and Neptune are also conjuncting in the midheaven. That suggests to me that in some way Kennedy was a
collective sacrifice. I am not sure that I would always interpret a
full eighth house as a violent death, because I have worked with

clients who have managed to carry a heavily tenanted eighth house into old age. But I would interpret a collision with the darker elements in the collective, which are of course inevitable in politics, but not everyone becomes the victim of them.

Another interesting example of outer planet houses heavily tenanted is Salvador Dali. Dali is a raving eccentric, which is a euphemism, and he is also the mouthpiece and chief exponent for the surrealist movement in art. In his chart the sun conjuncts Mercury and Mars in the eleventh house, while Pluto and Neptune fall in the twelfth. Surrealism has a strong ideological bias, and when it first burst upon the creative world it carried with it some

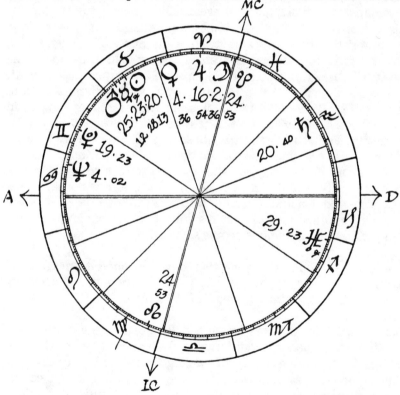

Illustration 8: BIRTH CHART OF SALVADOR DALI
May 11, 1904, 8:45 AM, Cadaques Garona, Spain
Source: Jones, Sabian Symbols

definite ideas about the world of the dream and the unconscious and the place of art in overturning concrete reality to open the way to the dreamworld. Dali and most of his compatriots were very influenced by Freud, and I think the whole movement has an Aquarian stamp because of this strongly structured and almost political bias.

There are innumerable other examples which I could use to illustrate this issue of heavily tenanted eighth, eleventh and twelfth houses. I think you get the picture. I would say that the operative word is movement, not in the sense of motion but a movement, a trend or powerful current of some kind that attracts or compels the individual and eventually becomes the ground for his personal fulfillment. Movements of this kind are in no way characteristic of the other houses or signs. Some of you are asking about particular people in history. Stalin had the sun in the twelfth house. I expected to find a sun-Pluto aspect in his chart, but there is none to be seen. But there is the mediumistic sun in the twelfth. Perhaps he was a medium for something at work in the collective body of Russia, just as Hitler was a medium for Germany. Perhaps his twelfth house sun says something about a violent catharsis that needed to occur in the nation. Someone asked about Edgar Cayce, who was a literal medium. He had Mercury, Saturn and Venus lined up in the eighth house. Someone also asked about Ghandi, who was another twelfth house sun, and another medium for his collective. We could go on like this for hours with famous people's charts.

Audience: I think it's interesting how the outer planets at the moment are passing through signs which are more collectively orientated, toward the latter part of the zodiac.

Liz: Yes, I think it's interesting too. The rest of the century will see them grouped in Sagittarius and Capricorn, with Pluto in Scorpio. I suppose one way of reading that would be to say that the major changes they are likely to precipitate concern collective institutions and mores, such as the legal system, religious movements, the monetary system, and so on.

Audience: Can you comment on what happens if the outer planets are retrograde in a birth chart?

Liz: I think that any retrograde planet tends to interiorise the expression of the planet. It operates on a more subjective and covert level. The meaning of the planet doesn't change, but its capacity for extroverted expression is altered. Retrograde planets have a very hard time telling you about themselves. For example, a retrograde Venus is just as orientated toward relationship, but it's very often a relationship with an idealised inner image of the person, and the actual partner often doesn't know very much about what is really going on. If Uranus is working on a more extroverted level, it will express through active changes and separations in life. But if you interiorise it, then it will begin to revolutionise one's thinking, and one's world of ideas may be very full of anarchistic or eccentric or advanced themes, but one's outer life may remain very conventional and staid. When Neptune exteriorises itself it will often make sacrifices for others, but if it interiorises then the issue of an inner mystical devotion and offering up of self becomes more important than loving gestures to the outside world. Pluto will seek power and change in the outer world, but if you introvert it then it becomes obsessive about altering the inner world. I would hesitate to say whether either of these is preferable. Nor do I think a couple of retrograde planets make a person introverted in Jung's sense of the word. But the planet itself works more on an interior level if it's retrograde.

Audience: Which house system are you using with these example charts?

Liz: They're all drawn up for Placidus house cusps. I prefer the quadrant systems to equal house because in the quadrant systems the axis of the MC and IC are the cusps of the tenth and fourth houses, and are emphasised in that way. The equal house system can give you something completely different on the cusps of the tenth and fourth, and the MC and IC float loose and seem to be unimportant. And I feel they are terribly important because they tell you a great deal about family inheritance and about the parents. As the tenth and fourth are the parental houses, it seems to me absurd to separate them from the midheaven axis.

This problem of house division is of course a long-standing problem. As with all other problems of this kind in astrology, I think you must work with various systems and choose the one which you feel works best for you. My orientation is much more psychological than that of many astrologers and I always pay careful attention to the family background. Perhaps that's not so relevant for other approaches to a chart, so an equal house chart might work on another level. But for me the keynote of the tenth house is the world. Mother is our first physical world, before we discover the bigger one outside, and the attitudes toward one shape the attitudes toward the other. Saturn as the natural ruler of the tenth is called the Lord of the World, and in Kabbalism it is the Great Mother. The midheaven is the cusp of the tenth house in quadrant systems, and is the point of inheritance from the mother as well as the obligations to the world.

I think you must simply do your charts by both systems for a while, if you have questions about this. Some people always do both, but I have abandoned using equal house because I'm not very happy with the information it reveals in terms of the psychology of the individual. I think you must also watch the progressions and transits in your own chart, to see, say, when something goes over a planet that might be either in the tenth or the ninth or the eleventh, to see what sphere of life is affected. That way you can gather your own evidence. I would be very hesitant to say that equal house is invalid and Placidus the only proper house system. But for my purposes I prefer Placidus.

Audience: Many textbooks say that the tenth house is the father and the fourth house the mother.

Liz: Yes, I know. That's yet another unsolvable problem. I think the tenth house represents the mother because in my experience that is who the house describes. By this I don't mean that planets in the tenth say what kind of person the mother is on a behavioural level. But I think the psychic inheritance from the mother is indicated. Very often it's her unconscious life that is represented, the unlived drives which were very strong in her but not properly expressed, which it then becomes the child's responsibility for carrying. Or you could also say that the planets in the tenth house describe the psychic image of the mother which we carry, which may not be wholly conscious and may not always correspond to how she acted. But if you dig a little into the person's deeper feelings about the mother and look for the traces in his relationships with women in general, you can see that the figure represented by the tenth house is very powerful in the person. The fourth house seems to me to say the same kind of thing about the father. It's the psychic inheritance of the father.

The point has been raised in various places that this connection of tenth with mother and fourth with father applies because of the particular parental structure in our society. That may be true, because in Western families not much is seen of the father, while the mother is omnipresent and is a much more powerful psychological force, not only because she gives birth to us and nurtures us at the beginning, but because she's often the only one there during most of childhood. I don't really know whether the tenth house is the mother or whichever parent happens to be playing the mother. Some people feel the latter is the case. Sometimes you see exceptions, but not very often. I think it would be a valid generalisation to say that the orientation of our culture is a patriarchal one, because law is so terribly important, as well as outer achievement. By this I don't mean that men rule us, in the way an extreme feminist would think. But both men and women in our society tend to give more value to intellectual achievement, material success, structured family life, a society governed by clearly defined laws and a hierarchical social system. This is perhaps a reflection of the religious values which have been dominant for us for many centuries, which are Judeo-Christian and which postulate the highest spiritual value as masculine.

I'm not suggesting that this is good or bad, because societies produce the values they need at any given time in history. But I think that this emphasis on one end of a pair results in the compensation of the unconscious in the other direction, just as in an individual too much emphasis on the intellect will cause an upheaval in the psyche from the feeling side. So the real psychological power in the home is wielded by the mother, whose value is less in the world's terms and therefore becomes greater in the unconscious. We are all horribly bound up with mother. I think this is why every person who propounds any kind of psychological theory places such enormous emphasis on her. She is huge for us in this culture, in a very unconscious way. Perhaps the tenth house represents the parent who is the strongest representative of one's fate, the thing which shapes the person. So mother is that person in a world structured as ours is. I don't know. These are just ideas. In actuality I think the tenth house is the mother because in my experience of reading charts, that is how it seems to come out.

If you do any work in counseling or psychotherapy, you very quickly discover the phenomenon of the absent father. Everyone seems to have an absent father. The father is the hidden parent, the one about whom least is known. But he is the source, and it's his name we carry. The fourth house is the hidden origin, the place from which we come, the seed of which we are a product. Father is so often a lost image in our world. He's away at work or off to war or preoccupied, or if he divorces or separates then mother gets the children and he has weekend visiting rights. We don't always know who father is. But we often have a surfeit of mother. She becomes Saturn for many people, the figure with the scythe who draws the limits of one's development and castrates or cuts down anything which tries to move beyond her. I wouldn't want to postulate the sociological reasons for this, because I am never sure how much is social conditioning and how much is archetypal and whether you can really separate them.

Audience: Can you comment on what happens when Jupiter is aspecting one of the outer planets?

Liz: Let's consider Jupiter first. I think that Jupiter is connected with the urge to believe in something, with faith and optimism in the future. Saturn is a bit like the stick with which the donkey is beaten from behind that gets him moving. But Jupiter is the carrot dangling in front of him that he's forever trying to reach. Jupiter says, "This could be better. You could be more than you are. You have potentials you haven't lived yet." Jupiter is concerned with what might be, rather than with what is. He's the character in the play who whispers in everyone else's ear that life could be a lot more interesting and what's a nice person like you still doing in a place like this?

When Jupiter is involved with the inner planets, then that spirit of optimism and the feeling of life as an adventure or a quest gets mixed up with very personal areas of life. Jupiter and Venus, for example, will together turn relationships into an adventure which can open up horizons for the person. Jupiter and Mercury will make learning and understanding a source of inspiration and adventure. When you put Jupiter with any of the personal planets, or in the signs that they rule, or their houses, then the ways in which the person will seek to expand and develop himself are fairly concrete and understandable and communicable.

But if you tie Jupiter up with the outer planets, then the road of development and adventure and meaning leads away from the purely personal and into a much larger life. The human family as a collective whole becomes the adventure, and it's a lot harder to articulate that in a way which is comprehensible. Jupiter together with Uranus, for example, or in Aquarius, or in the eleventh, opens up the whole panorama of human evolution and social development and the growth of consciousness. It isn't just your ideas, or my ideas, it's the world of ideas and their development through history. Or if you place Jupiter with Neptune, or in Pisces, or in the twelfth, it's not so much a personal religious search that attracts you, but rather the vast theatre of religious yearning as a whole, and the experience of human suffering and whatever meaning there might be in it. You can see that Jupiter bound up with Neptune gets contaminated, in a way, with *the* religious spirit, rather than just your religious aspirations. Jupiter in the twelfth house is a kind of mediator for the spiritual longings of the collective, and that can place a burden on the person who has it there because he immediately wants to help everybody. The sense of shared suffering and shared longing for grace and redemption will often push the person into a vocation which deals with people's pain. Sometimes these are the individuals who devote a lifetime to caring for ailing parents, or sacrifice a great deal of their own personal satisfaction because of that sense of human despair and longing.

The problem with Jupiter in this context is that it's very easy to lose the sense of one's own boundaries. There is a tendency to forget that one person cannot heal mankind, or understand everything about human development, or carry everybody's shadow. Some clarity is needed, because Jupiter inflates and sees hopeful visions which aren't always able to be achieved. I think we can learn a great deal from the meaning of the houses and signs opposite those three collective ones. Leo and the fifth house are opposite Aquarius and the eleventh, so the balance to getting completely lost in an idea of the perfect social order and the perfect humanity is a little healthy selfishness and self-indulgence. Virgo and the sixth house are opposite Pisces and the twelfth, so the antidote to crucifying yourself in the name of alleviating other people's pain is a sense of physical boundaries and time and space and a recognition of limits. Taurus and the second house are opposite Scorpio and the eighth, and the thing which offsets drowning in the murk of other people's and one's own repressed desires and aggression and passions is a good sense of your own tastes, values, and the need for some permanence and security in your material life.

Someone asked earlier about Saturn in the twelfth house. One of the things that I think Saturn represents is the defense system of the organism. It's our skin, the psychic organ which structures and draws boundaries and protects and shuts out harmful or threatening experience. I think Saturn in the twelfth is terribly sensitive to the chaotic unconscious dream-world of the collective, but the person finds it terrifying and tries to defend himself against it, either by walling it out altogether or trying to formulate it into definite, manageable, safe tools. The house in which Saturn falls is the arena of life where you have the most fear, the most insecurity, and also, on a better note, the most determination to become self-sufficient and conquer the frightening thing. In some ways a twelfth house Saturn is an excellent position for exploration of the inner world, because it's so careful and cautious. But sometimes I have seen people who project the frightening forces of the collective onto external institutions and groups, and then they become very busy defending themselves from something they imagine is in the outside world. Obviously that can lead to a lot of trouble with authorities and so on.

I spoke earlier about Hitler with his twelfth house Uranus. I think the receptivity to collective currents of ideas is enhanced when Uranus is in the twelfth. One picks up things that are around, as if there were a radio antenna picking up all the latest broadcasts. I've noticed that a twelfth house Uranus is often full of ideas and intuitions of a political kind, what's going to happen in the world and who's going to do what to which country. And very often these intuitions are accurate. This can be a gift, but as with all the outer planets there must be some strong sense of who you are as an individual, as well as a realistic observation of what the world is actually like at the moment. Otherwise one just gets carried away, and the next movement that comes along takes you with it. Whether you were right or not about your political visions becomes rather irrelevant.

Audience: What about Pluto in the twelfth house?

Liz: I think this has something to do with sensitivity to the dark in the collective. It's rather paranoid. Planets in the twelfth house tend to lie about very unconsciously. One isn't aware of carrying them most of the time. A twelfth house Pluto is very open to the primitive drives in the collective, which are as you may imagine not always pleasing and attractive. But usually there is only a vague sense of unease around crowds, or a fear of groups. Pluto has a tendency to erupt, however, and then it can be very disturbing, because you may have a bad attack of agoraphobia or claustrophobia, or people suddenly become very threatening when there are more than three of them in a room, or the dark element floods the ego and the person begins to behave in a very dictatorial or explosive fashion. If a person with Pluto in the twelfth spends a lot of time around groups, he is liable to pick up the unconscious undertow, especially if there is a lot of repressed aggression or resentment. Then the person will suddenly erupt and start behaving badly, because he's acting out all the emotional murk that everyone else has sat on. And of course he gets blamed, and feels terrible because something just came over him. I have noticed this particularly with groups which are very civilised and good and nice and full of well-motivated helpful people. Planets in the twelfth house smell out everything that is not revealed which is being carried around by the group, and Pluto in particular will pick up the primitive.

There is another interesting area connected with the outer planets which I would like to talk about now. This deals with the qualities of masculine and feminine which they represent. The outer planets when they are experienced as images in dreams and fantasies have a very mythical cast. Venus, for example, is a warm, human, accessible woman, and will often wear the face of someone that you love. But Neptune and Pluto are not human and accessible. They're collective and their images are very impersonal and archetypal. They might be the Virgin Mary, or the Terrible Dragon. Those are images which are universal to mankind, and don't bear the personal stamp of one's own individual experience and feeling.

I think we are all affected in terms of our images of male and female by the kind of parents we had. A woman's first experience of men is of course her father, and her gradually developing image of the masculine is in part coloured by what kind of father she had. This means not only how he behaved, but what he was underneath, his unconscious life as well. The first woman a man meets is his mother, and his image of the feminine is strongly coloured by the maternal experience. You can also say that a woman will model her femininity in the beginning after the mother, and a man will model his masculinity after his father. This is an unconscious process, and it happens when we are very young. There is also a component in these images of masculine and feminine which is highly individual, and doesn't spring from the environment or the parents. This is what is in your own birth chart. The sun and moon, and Venus and Mars, describe to a great extent what our own individual experiences of male and female are, inside and outside.

These two components overlap. There is a mystery in that, because what you have in your own horoscope belongs to you, and is part of your own pattern of development, but often the parents are described very specifically, as if there were a co-incidence of inner and outer images. So your experience of mother through the moon and Venus and the tenth house is not only your own, but also your mother's. Your experience of father through the sun and Mars and the fourth house is not only your actual father but the father principle in yourself, and your image of father in the world. The women and men in one's life, whether mother or sister or nanny or adolescent love or husband or wife, bear the stamp of the qualities which are there in the chart in the beginning.

This is the personal aspect of the image of masculine and feminine. There's also a collective component to these images. There is a level where a universal experience of man and woman lies below the highly distinctive individualised one. We each have our own personal attractions and dislikes and tastes in the matter of what qualities of male and female we encounter. One man might please me while another will repel me. None of us fall in love with everybody. There is a boundary line, just as there is a line drawn on the map of the mountains which I put on the blackboard at the beginning. Below that line the distinctive differences start merging, and there are basic archetypal attributes which belong to male and female which are inherent in the human experience.

I think the outer planets are related to these archetypal images, which are very potent and profound and often terrifying. You can meet them in many dreams, and they are far more numinous and disturbing than the dream-figures which belong to our personal lives. Sometimes a person will become obsessed with this kind of image, and then he cannot possibly form a relationship with another individual, because he is forever looking for the archetypal figure. No human being is satisfactory. I saw a rather disturbing film recently called *Bad Timing*, and the woman portrayed in the film is a very classic anima type as Jung might describe it. She is elusive and unpredictable, unpossessable, erotic, destructive, eternally enticing, eternally chaotic. She isn't an individual woman, but an image of the feminine in its most alluring and dangerous form. She's the sort of hysterical, disintegrated anima type that John Fowles writes about in *The French Lieutenant's Woman*. If a film director manages to successfully portray this kind of collective image, then the film affects people very powerfully. Or if an author catches these qualities then his book will appeal to a mass reading audience, because this kind of figure is universal in the collective unconscious. She's eternally enticing to men, and many women are caught by her and act her out, and lose their own individual souls in the process.

When we experience these figures in our lives, then our dialogue about them becomes very predictable. After you have heard a few hundred people describe exactly the same situation, you begin to wonder if there isn't a factory hidden away somewhere where these behaviour patterns are manufactured. The rather hysterical woman I described before is very Neptunian. She isn't the only face of Neptune, but she's a very characteristic one. The compassionate and spiritually redeeming woman is another face of Neptune, and the collective has found its best image of her in the cult of Mary.

There are characteristic archetypal masculine images as well. Once again, they are the meat of films and novels. The current antihero is I think a characteristically Uranian figure. Uranus is a sort of embodiment of the logos principle. He rules through mind, not through brawn, and often he's so abstract that he becomes a machine, or an invisible god. He's the principle of will, cold, clear, decisive, and impersonal. He's also the winged god, the creative, aspiring spirit which can't be contained or possessed, but which alights for a while and then goes on his way.

You can see that if a person has Venus strongly aspected to Uranus or Neptune or Pluto then the experience of love and relationship gets coloured by these more mythical images. The ordinary happy married life that our society upholds is often just not enough for the person, because he is chasing after some transpersonal or mythical experience through love. Archetypal images always seem more glamourous than actual people. Of course the fact that they don't exist in embodied form causes some problems, but the pursuit continues. You can see this problem very often with moon-Neptune or Venus-Neptune in a man's chart. He will tend to seek a very idealised image of woman, who is a sort of cross between a siren and the Virgin, and who doesn't present him with terrible human foibles like headaches, period cramps and emotional demands. The mystical vision of woman is much more enchanting to him than the actual one, in part because it can't be possessed and therefore never disappoints or pushes him into actual life through responsibilities and feelings.

These aspects in both men's and women's charts explain a good deal of the sort of problems that erupt despite the best intentions in relationships. The experience of the collective image is an important and valid one, but it's not very productive when one demands that it be embodied by a single individual. It can dominate the early part of life and then it's usually justifiable, but pursuit of it in tangible form in later life is often very unhappy and disillusioning and desperate. Sometimes it's a creative form that the image needs, and in many ways the portrayal of it through films and novels is a way in which both the artist and his audience can have a collective experience without too many individual lives being shattered pointlessly. At the very least, understanding that these planets describe inner states rather than people can give some meaning to the difficulties that one experiences in relationships through them.

The ways in which creative people have given expression to these outer planets is extremely interesting. Goethe is a good example, because of his creation of Faust. Goethe had a sun-Pluto square in his birth chart. He also had a Scorpio ascendant, so the Plutonian element in the chart is very emphasised. I mentioned Jimmy Carter earlier, who had this same square, and also Margaret Thatcher. Both of these people found political arenas in which to both express and battle with Pluto. But Goethe chose to create a work of art which is truly Plutonian. Faust embodies the whole spectrum of power and darkness and dismemberment and salvation that are contained in Pluto. I have always thought that Plutonian people never made very good Christians, because Pluto's combination of God and the devil is more akin to gnosticism or dualism than it is to Christianity. How much Goethe was able to work off through his art and how much he was tormented himself by Pluto I couldn't say. But he has given us a monumental creation that encapsulates what I understand to be the conflict of opposites contained in that planet.

Another good example is Chopin. He had the sun in Pisces in square to Neptune. Chopin's music is to me an embodiment of Neptunian pathos and melancholy and longing and delicacy. Wagner is also an interesting example. He had the sun opposite Uranus. The mythology of *The Ring* is thinly disguised political ideology—the gods are degenerate and dying, and man must become god for the new society to be born. Madame Blavatsky, who founded the Theosophical Society, is another sun opposite Uranus. The impeccably organised vision of the cosmos which she perpetrated is characteristically Uranian. Although Theosophy isn't very popular anymore and those with a bent in that direction prefer more psychologically sophisticated terminology, nevertheless we astrologers owe a good deal to Madame Blavatsky. It was the Theosophists who unearthed astrology and dusted it off and brought it back into the modern world.

There are any number of excellent examples of well-known people who have expressed their dilemma with an outer planet through creating some artistic or political or psychological vessel through which the energy can be expressed. I mentioned Jung and Freud earlier. The list is endless. I hope that this illustrates the way in which the outer planets can seize a person and compel him to follow them, either creatively or destructively, into some kind of wider vision. I don't think that because the sun doesn't aspect Uranus, Neptune or Pluto, that this possibility is denied a person. There is no such thing as a chart without these planets, and they are going to express through some area of the individual's life. The danger is in not knowing what they want, or in trying to shut them out, because then one tends to become their victim rather than their co-operative vessel.

Someone has asked if I would comment on the Jupiter-Saturn conjunction and whether this has any bearing on the situation between America and Iran. Jupiter and Saturn come into con-

junction in December of this year* in around seven or eight degrees of Libra. The conjunction continues through January,
February and March, and back and forth during the whole of
1981. These are of course not outer planets, and in a sense they
don't belong in this conference, but everyone seems a bit worried
about the conjunction here so I suppose I should try to sound
intelligent about it. One of the things which other astrologers
have noted about Jupiter-Saturn cycles is that they coincide with
important economic fluctuations such as sudden rises and depres-
sions in the stock market. There is also the curious phenomenon
of American presidents dying in office who have been elected
under Jupiter-Saturn conjunctions since they have occurred in
earth signs. I think in many ways it might be more relevant and
interesting in the context of this workshop to talk about the
conjunction in relation to the charts of particular countries.
Talking about the meaning of the conjunction would be fascinating but its effect on specific trouble spots is even more fascinating. Usually if a country's chart is affected by Jupiter-Saturn it
will be through the economy. Or the rulership changes, which is
the old meaning of Jupiter-Saturn as it was interpreted in the
Middle Ages. Something old and outworn is dethroned and there
is a burst of new energy and some chaos before a new, younger
thing emerges.

The three charts which I think might be worth looking at are
those of America, Iran and Israel. I was also going to talk about
Russia's horoscope, which I will do shortly. I'm not an expert in
mundane astrology, and my tendency is to look at a country's
chart psychologically, in the same way that I would look at an
individual's. So I cannot make concrete predictions that will help
anybody invest money at the right time. I think there are other
astrologers who have made more of a speciality of this field, which
is certainly a worthwhile one to examine. There is also the problem of the accuracy of these national horoscopes. Israel, for
example, is given two quite different charts according to the two
source books I have looked at. The one which has ten degrees of
Libra rising, which I will be using, is based on the data given in
the *Times* when the state was proclaimed in 1948. This chart
appears in Charles Carter's book on political astrology. There is

---

*1980.

another chart which gives a one degree Scorpio ascendant which has been calculated by the American Federation of Astrologers. I don't know which is accurate. The same problem occurs with America's chart, because of the uncertainty of the time of the signing of the Declaration of Independence. I have used the chart Dane Rudhyar gives in his book on America's astrology. Iran's chart is a dog's breakfast, because when a country changes form as drastically as Iran has, then it is in a sense born anew. But from what moment should one date the birth of Khomeini's Iran? From the moment his foot was placed on Iranian soil? Or the moment of the collapse of the Shah's government? You can see the problems with national charts. Nevertheless it's worth commenting on, if for no other reason than to open up speculation and illustrate the way in which a nation is a collective entity with its own psyche. A nation is born at a particular moment, although it might be a little difficult to get the information, and it embodies a particular pattern of development in the same way that an individual does. It has a fate and a bias of temperament and conflicts and insecurities and gifts and potentials, and the psychic mechanisms such as compensation that are at work in individuals are also at work in nations. Nations also project parts of their charts just as people do, and elect another nation to become the carrier of one end of a natal square.

I'll begin with America because even with the problem over the time of birth, at least there is agreement about the day and therefore we can see what the Jupiter-Saturn transit in Libra will do to the natal planets. I am personally convinced by Rudhyar's chart because it seems to me to describe what I see very accurately. Saturn is in the tenth house in Libra, and the midheaven is around two degrees of Libra. Saturn falls in square to the natal Jupiter-sun conjunction in Cancer in the seventh house, which deals with the other whether it's another person or another country. The tenth house in mundane charts always refers to the style of government, the leader, just as in an individual chart it is the person's image or persona in the eyes of the world, the thing which rules him in terms of external standards of behaviour.

Now, the Jupiter-Saturn conjunction lands on the midheaven-Saturn midpoint, and hovers around Saturn for quite some time. That suggests some turmoil in terms not only of the present government, which would be very unlikely to survive another term in office after a transit like this, but it also suggests to me that

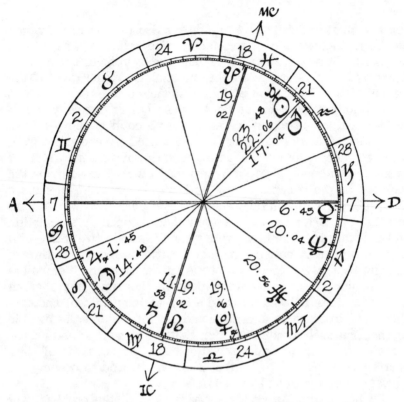

Illustration 10: BIRTH CHART OF THE ISLAMIC REPUBLIC
OF IRAN (Khomeini)
February 11, 1979, 2:00 PM, Teheran, Iran
Source: Moore, The Book of World Horoscopes

America's image of authority and rule in the world might take a
bit of buffeting. Saturn in Libra tends to set itself up as the
arbiter of rights, the fair judge and leader and guide. That is of
course the role America has played for a long time in terms of
presenting itself this way to other nations. This transit is of
course a Saturn return as well as a Jupiter-Saturn conjunction,
so there would be a maturing process at work, a growing up
through limitations or difficulties or even humiliation of some
kind which would make the country more realistic about itself
and its position.

The fact that the transit stirs up the natal squares suggests to

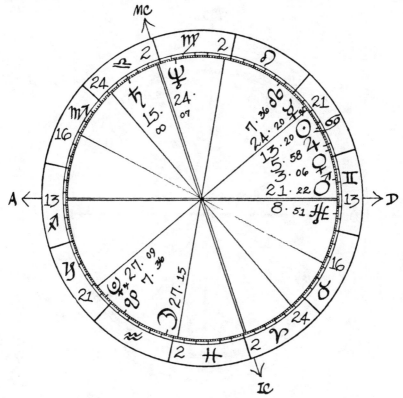

Illustration 11: BIRTH CHART OF THE USA
 July 4, 1776, 5:00 PM, Philadelphia, Pennsylvania
Source: Rudhyar, The Astrology of America's Destiny

me that the conflict might erupt through a collision with another country. Although this does not have to mean a war, it is certainly a confrontation. Saturn in square to the sun in a person's chart suggests a deep sense of inadequacy and insecurity, and a need to prove oneself over and over again to others. I would say the same thing about the aspect appearing in a national psyche. It is a defensive aspect, and when Jupiter is thrown in it can become boastful and self-aggrandising in order to mask the feelings of doubt. Obviously this kind of configuration has its creative side, because it forces growth and fosters a determination to succeed. It's just that there is a kind of obsessiveness about the growth. So this is

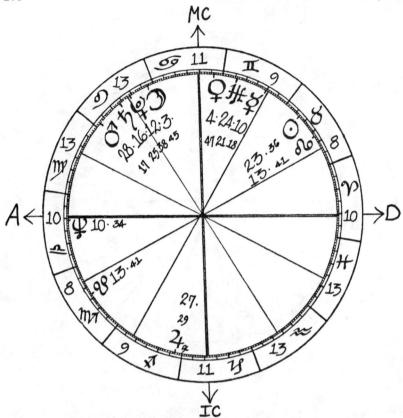

Illustration 9: BIRTH CHART OF ISRAEL
May 14, 1948, 4:00 PM, Tel Aviv
Source: Carter, Introduction to Political Astrology

the basic psychic pattern which the transiting Jupiter-Saturn conjunction will trigger. There are implications of an overestimation of something in relation to another country, and a blow to the image or the national pride, and a re-evaluation of standards and goals as a result.

The Jupiter-Saturn conjunction falls on the ascendant of Israel's chart. It also conjuncts the natal Neptune, which is in ten degrees of Libra in both Carter's and the AFA charts. Saturn, I should mention, will be hanging about in the first half of Libra long after Jupiter has moved on, so the effects of this transit will probably last for quite a while, through the first half of 1982 at least. Jupiter and Saturn moving over the ascendant suggests to me that it is the personal identity of the nation which is being affected. The ascendant is the thing toward which we aspire, the myth which we try to live. We may not be equipped to live it very well because the rest of the chart may contradict it, but we will try nevertheless. The Sagittarian ascendant in America's chart seems to me to be much more descriptive than the usual Gemini ascendant given, because the dream of the American is the life of the free individual with space to roam in and his own autonomy over his own lifestyle. Sagittarius is a cowboy at heart, whereas Gemini is a cultured intellectual—not the thing I would associate with the image of the typical American as he presents himself to the world.*

So Israel sees itself as either a Libran or a Scorpio, depending upon which chart you prefer. I can't really assess this, because I have never lived there and have no direct experience of the nation. Libra is an idealistic sign, and despite the various encounters Israel has had with its neighbours in the years since it was founded, I think there has always been an attempt to present itself as a place where a formerly persecuted people can live in peace and without threat. The ideal of Israel is a great dream, and I think there is a case to be made for that Libran ascendant with its hope of an orderly, beautiful, harmonious life. The transit of Saturn over this point, which means over Neptune as well, suggests a disillusionment, a recognition of the fact that the world might not be like that. Saturn transiting over Neptune in an individual's chart has a very disillusioning effect, because some great dream or fantasy that has always been cherished tends to take a battering from material reality. If the fantasy has any truth in it, it is left more realistic, and if it's just wild, then it collapses altogether. Jupiter makes things want to grow, but Saturn curtails the growth through harsh reality.

The effect of this conjunction on a country is going to be much the same as the effect on an individual. If you have an ascendant somewhere within orb of the seven or eight degree point of the conjunction, then Jupiter will bring out the need to open up your life, to develop yourself either through relationships or through separating from relationships. But Saturn promotes the realisation that you are limited by circumstances and by your own fears and blockages. Saturn forces a confrontation with responsibility, with what hasn't been done or sorted out. The

---

*Ed. Note: Barry Lynes, in his books *The Next 20 Years* and *Astroeconomics*, presents extensive research supporting a USA chart with Sagittarius rising. Lynes' impressive work draws the conclusion that an Ascendant of 7° Sagittarius correlates most precisely with both transits and historical events. Write the publisher of this book for information on Mr. Lynes' works.

vision of a free future arises just at the moment when you are feeling most inadequate and least able to manifest it. The reaction of course varies. You can try to put the two things together, and use the vision as a goal toward which to work, taking care of what needs to be looked at internally or externally. That would be a more creative way of reacting. Or you can overcompensate and get terribly restless because of the feeling of restriction, and start blaming everything and everyone in sight for the fact that you can't have this beautiful thing you suddenly realise you want.

Of course an individual has options which a country doesn't, because an individual can bring his consciousness to bear on a problem. A nation must react, because the mass is a very unconscious organism, and the less individual the people are in a nation, the more wildly it will react to planetary pressure. If I saw the squares between Saturn and Jupiter conjunct sun in America's horoscope in a person's chart, linking the seventh and tenth houses as they do, I would probably suggest that the person try some analysis to get at the root of the insecurities that make him behave so compulsively. But a country unfortunately can't go into analysis. The blinder and more indoctrinated the people are in a country, the more hysterical their responses are likely to be when a sensitive point gets triggered. But a people don't become more conscious except by each individual coming to terms with his own issues. That is very difficult, and is the thing most of us would rather avoid dealing with. It's far easier to go along with whatever is happening and then get very angry when a country like Iran misbehaves. Or, on the other hand, if you're Iranian, to get very angry if America misbehaves.

The chart for Iran which I have put up on the board is set for the collapse of the Shah's government and the establishment of the Islamic Republic under Khomeini. I have no idea whether it's a correct chart or not. That's the problem with many of these mundane horoscopes, because sources conflict. This chart gives an ascendant of seven degrees of Cancer, with Venus in seven Capricorn on the descendant. The Jupiter-Saturn conjunction would therefore square both the ascendant and the natal Venus. A square to the ascendant is much like a conjunction, but it's more aggressive and unpredictable. So the things I said about the Jupiter-Saturn over Israel's ascendant would apply here, about the urge for sudden expansion and perhaps rather inflationary ideas about the country's own importance, coupled with a sharp backlash either from hostile neighbours or from internal stress. If I were going to visualise a myth about the Cancer ascendant, I would use words like tradition and return to the roots, and also I would think of a clannish, introverted, self-contained entity which tried to create a culture based on a fantasy of the glorious past. I would expect hypersensitivity to criticism and a strong national feeling of a family rather than a political entity. I think all these things are true about the new Iran. The square to Venus at the descendant from the transiting Jupiter-Saturn certainly suggests trouble with previously friendly countries, and a disillusionment which is typical of Saturn-Venus about just who are one's friends and enemies.

While I enjoy speculating about the effects of the transit in the charts of countries, I am not totally happy about the accuracy of the ascendants in these charts, which makes me rather reluctant to talk in other than general terms. I would on a concrete level expect some sort of embarrassment or humiliation for the American government because of the tenth house Saturn, and I would expect Iran to get involved in a scrap of some kind with a neighbour, perhaps Israel, although there are other Muslim countries who do not like Khomeini. That is as far as I would wish to go. I suppose also that I am not unduly alarmed by Jupiter-Saturn, because neither is an outer planet and the forces which are unleashed in the collective are not so terrifying or overwhelming as those which the outer planets represent. If the Jupiter-Saturn affects your own chart, then you must find your own solution to the problem of a sudden burgeoning of hope and enthusiasm and sense of new possibilities, coupled with a restriction or problem that prevents that hope from materialising.

Audience: Can you say something about the chart for Great Britain?

Liz: Yes, but I am worried about spending a great deal of time on these national charts at this point. There is the same problem here as to which chart is correct. There is a chart for England, based on the crowning of William the Conqueror, which gives the sun in Capricorn at the midheaven and an Aries ascendant. Kings were traditionally crowned at noon when the sun was at the zenith so the time is probably accurate. There is also a chart for the United Kingdom, which is the incorporation of Scotland and Wales, and

Northern Ireland, and interestingly this too gives the sun in Capricorn, with a Libran ascendant. The ascendant is seven degrees of Libra, so the Jupiter-Saturn conjunction would land on it in the same way that it lands on the ascendant of Israel. There is a third chart for Great Britain which represents the union of England and Scotland in 1707, and that has the sun in Taurus with a sixteen degree Capricorn ascendant. One thing is apparent, which is the dominance of Capricorn in all three horoscopes.

Now I realise the difficulty in offering generalisations about a country, because people will always stand up and say that it's different in their village and so on. But as I was not born in England, I have a slightly more unjaundiced view of it from the outside, and the Capricornian qualities are very apparent to me. Although the English forever protest that they are no longer a class-structured society, they of course are precisely that, and any American who has been born in a genuinely class-free country is struck by the class distinctions, no matter how hard people protest against them. It's deeply embedded in the British psyche. Capricorn is a hierarchical sign, and firmly believes that everything has its appropriate place. It's a deeply conservative sign, and I mean the word in its broad sense, not in its specifically political one. A taxi driver was quoted recently in the *Times* as describing what he felt to be the basic British attitude toward life. He said, "If it moves, club it to death." Put euphemistically, that means a certain caution about new and progressive elements. Ideas and products which are quickly taken up in America and Germany and Holland eventually seep into England twenty years later. That is terribly Capricornian. So is the incredible solidity and determination and doggedness, which only becomes apparent when a war or some other disaster shakes people out of their muddling-through approach. Then the Capricorn spine of stainless steel shows itself.

Audience: I suppose things will get shaken up quite a bit when Uranus and Neptune move into Capricorn.

Liz: Yes, I was building up to talking about that transit. That was going to come later. But yes, I would expect quite a shakeup. I think the strongly Capricornian feeling here is very difficult for many fiery types, who find it restrictive and oppressive. Other people who are fiery or lack earth find the opposite, that it's a very stabilising place, because you simply can't extend beyond a certain limit. If nothing else, the weather stops you. The physical and psychic climate foster introversion. In a place like California, or Australia, the beauty of the climate and the open space bring people out of themselves into a much more physical and extroverted existence. But an English winter drives you into yourself, which is frightening for some people and very creative for others. Things must be grounded in England, properly rooted, or they die. You can't live on potential and promises in the way you can in many American cities. In this way a country affects an individual, just as an individual affects a country.

You can do a synastry between your own chart and the chart of a nation, if you can obtain it, and see where your own values might agree or conflict with, say, the style of government or the mythic vision of that country. It's possible to begin to take these charts quite seriously, and to see that the world is a series of intricately interconnected psychic entities, some large and some small, none of which are wholly independent of or unaffected by the others. A country has its birth according to the birth of the constitution which states its form and its laws. Some countries have several charts. France, for example, has undergone many metamorphoses. Initially it was a kingdom, but the kingdom was much smaller than modern France and was surrounded by independent duchies and fiefs of the Holy Roman Empire. It's had a series of republics, and it has had an emperor. The political entity which we now know as France would have to be assessed by the horoscope for the Fifth or Gaullist Republic, because that forms the constitutional basis for modern France. The Iranian chart on the board is Khomeini's Iran, which is very different from the Shah's Iran. But each state is a living entity, which has its own psychic laws.

It also becomes possible to get a glimpse of why nations line up on a particular side of the fence against other nations. They are attracted to and recoil from each other just like people do. The charts of national rulers also link up with one another, which is not surprising, and it contributes to why Jimmy Carter might get on with Margaret Thatcher and not with Khomeini. With all the interlocking aspects which one finds between the charts of nations and the charts of rulers, it isn't surprising that a transit which triggers one will trigger another. National charts are as psychological as individual ones. America's sun-Saturn square is no less inner than a person's, and no less indicative of deep feelings of inadequacy and deep compulsions for achievement in compensation.

Uranus, Neptune and Pluto can also be seen similarly in a national chart. I think they represent deeply unconscious collective movements which erupt through the houses in which they are placed, just as the inner planets represent the more conscious values and goals of a nation and a person. Israel has a Saturn-Pluto conjunction, which suggests the same kind of internal conflict with the shadow side of life as I would interpret in an individual's Saturn-Pluto conjunction. But countries have less freedom, because they are expressive of the psyches of millions of individuals operating through the basic framework of the national chart, and of those millions of individuals a not very sizable proportion take time to reflect on their own actions and feelings and attitudes.

Audience: What about the points where people like Hitler appear who alter a country's destiny? Does that show in the transits and progressions to a country's chart?

Liz: I think it's a bit like the times when major changes are happening in a person and a significant figure appears either in the dream life or outside. Transits and progressions reflect changes in consciousness, and herald new things emerging into life. Those kinds of changes are personified, or condensed to use Freud's word, into a particular image or figure which is a symbol for the new energy or change. I think an important political, religious or artistic figure appears in a country's life in exactly the same way, who reflects or embodies the thing which is trying to emerge from the collective. You can see this process very clearly if you observe the patterns of dreams. A particular kind of figure may suddenly begin to appear in the dreams when everything in external life seems relatively peaceful and quiet. A thief steals something, or a black man climbs in through the window, or a mysterious woman begins to beckon the dreamer. Then a few nights later the same motif is repeated, although the form may change slightly. If a motif keeps repeating like that, then it implies that some new psychic content is getting ready to enter the person's awareness and his life. This may occur as an inner change, or it may synchronise with an actual individual appearing on the scene who is the catalyst for the person undergoing change. I think a person appearing in the context of national destiny serves exactly the same role. Hitler was a catalyst, an embodiment of something already at work in the depths of the German psyche. This something found the right mouthpiece, as it always seems to do. If Jimmy Carter blunders in his role as President of the United States and gets the country into an embarrassing or dangerous political situation, then that will coincide with transits across the country's chart which necessitate this kind of experience. Then the people elect exactly the right leader to fulfill the need. The leader's chart is usually strongly connected to the country's chart, and the same transit hits them both.

Audience: Most sources give Gemini as the American ascendant. Why do you feel it's Sagittarius?

Liz: I didn't come up with that ascendant, Dane Rudhyar did. I am reacting on a purely subjective and intuitive basis when I say that I feel Sagittarius is much more appropriate. I think the ascendant concerns things like the image, of a person or a country, and the vision of that person or country in terms of what they are striving to become. You run into it everywhere. I have always associated Gemini with intellectual gifts, because it's an airy sign. Gemini when it's being typical is a model of dilettante culture. Love of learning and scholarship, love of language and the artful uses of it, subtle wit, polish and sophistication are all traits I connect with Gemini. I am afraid this is just not the image of the typical American. Of course there is no such thing as a typical American, because it's a huge country with many different environments and cultural influences. But there is a myth of the typical American, which you can see on any television commercial. That mythic image permeates all sorts of things. Sagittarius on the other hand is a much more active, energetic sign than Gemini. Its cry is always freedom and individuality. Sagittarius is a homegrown philosopher, with homely sayings about life, not an erudite wit who can quote Voltaire and Heraclitus at you. It's a bit of a cowboy, in love with the open spaces and with physical fitness and stamina. It's a big sign in every way, always striving to get bigger. It's religious in a rather indiscriminating and sometimes bigoted way, with a great heart but not very much subtlety. I think all those qualities are typical of the myth of the American. I can think of no country in the world which houses as many different religions, yet which is as peculiarly narrow and bigoted in its religious outlook.

Audience: Even California?

Liz: Particularly California. Each one of the hundred thousand cults and sects in California has the right to exist and hates all the other ninety-nine thousand and ninety-nine. But the thing about Sagittarius is the tremendous optimism and religious spirit. Everything is in the name of God and country, God being first but naturally assumed to be on the country's side in any event. The American myth is embodied in the cowboy. That's not Gemini. By no stretch of the imagination can you turn sophisticated Gemini into a cowboy, except at a fancy-dress party when he can act the role beautifully for twenty minutes.

As I warned you earlier, I'm not an expert on mundane or judicial astrology. I'm mainly interested in it from the point of view of the psychology behind political movements. But mundane astrology has until this century always had a very high place in astrological history. Modern astrology is no longer a unity which studies all branches. It has split up, so that there is an area where statistical correlations are more important and an area where psychology is more important, and so on. That is perhaps necessary now. We are much more specialised and differentiated than we were five hundred years ago. But the charts of nations were as important as the charts of individuals once upon a time, and the same dynamics have always applied to both. If Jupiter conjunct Saturn arrives on your natal tenth house Saturn and you get into a dreadful scrape with your colleagues at work and you wind up being made to look very silly and have to re-evaluate your capacities and mistakes, that is no different to what America feels under the same transit. The only difference is in the size of the entity, and perhaps in the deadliness or potential constructiveness of the reactions on a grander scale. And if you don't have a Jupiter-Saturn transit but your country does, and your country goes hysterical in reaction, you can begin to see that perhaps you don't have to go hysterical too.

Lecture Five

I wanted to talk for a bit about Russia's horoscope, and then I would like to go into the conjunctions of the outer planets which are approaching in the next two decades, which seem to be frightening everybody so much. This chart is given by the AFA for the time of the Bolshevik Revolution and the taking of power by Lenin. Once again, I cannot guarantee the accuracy of the ascendant because I doubt that anyone stood by with a stopwatch, but the placements of the planets are accurate and they are extremely interesting.*

It's probably worth mentioning, or repeating, that this horoscope represents a political entity rather than the "soul of the nation" as some people describe the qualities of a people. The things which we all imaginatively attribute to different nationalities as basic characteristics are I think very different from this kind of horoscope. The psychological qualities of a people cannot be mapped, because you cannot find a birth time when that people was born. I suppose if you want to think in more mystical terms, it's a bit like the dichotomy between a person's birth chart and his soul or Self, which is a great mystery and is most certainly not in the birth chart. My fantasy is that the soul of a nation or a people will undergo a series of incarnations, which are represented by the different governments and birth horoscopes of nations. So what we are looking at is not Mother Russia as her people feel about her, but a political entity which was born on 7 November 1917 in accordance with certain ideological precepts. Perhaps this is one of the incarnations of the soul of Mother Russia. Perhaps it isn't the last one either. Nations have lifespans too. No nation continues forever in the same form, although some are much longer lived than others. I think that a nation's chart also suggests the depth and stubbornness of its conflicts. Whenever I see configurations involving the fixed signs in an individual chart, such as a T-cross or a grand cross, I am left with the impression that these issues are very deeply embedded in the individual's character. Perhaps they are issues which have been in the family psyche for many generations. There is a sense of immense solidity both to the character and to its problems, and any changes that the person tries to make in terms of character take a very long time and move

---

*Ed. Note: Barry Lynes' extensive research on the natal chart of the USSR results in a chart with 26°50' Virgo rising, drawn for Nov. 8, 1917 at Petrograd. Numerous USSR charts are hypothecized due to the chaos at that time.

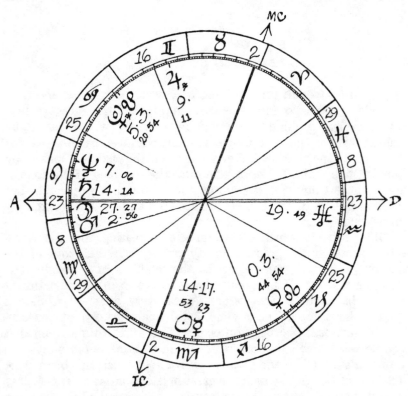

Illustration 12: BIRTH CHART OF THE USSR
November 7, 1917, 10:52 PM, Leningrad
Source: Moore, The Book of World Horoscopes

very slowly. Configurations involving cardinal and mutable signs, on the other hand, can shift their expression rather dramatically.

One of the most noticeable things in the Russian chart is the conjunction of Saturn and Neptune in Leo, and the opposition of Saturn to Uranus in Aquarius. I spoke earlier about contacts of Saturn with the outer planets as having a quality of compulsiveness, because the powerful undercurrents arising from the collective psyche break through and threaten the shell of the ego, forcing the person to do something actively with the pressure. Now Saturn-Neptune has the flavour of a mystical vision, a religious longing. In Leo it has a peculiarly autocratic flavour.

Saturn-Neptune in Leo would say something like, "I am God's emissary on earth, destined to bring you the One Truth which will overcome all evil and create the perfect kingdom of God on earth." There is a very strong sense of one's own inner divinity with this conjunction in Leo, and that can be very creative in an individual if there are suitable outlets for the urge. It's a bit trickier with a country, because you can at least argue with a Saturn-Neptune person who is convinced that he is always and ultimately right. Interestingly this conjunction falls in Russia's twelfth house, where it hides in the depths of the unconscious. It's a kind of ancestral vestige of the days of the czars.

Saturn in opposition to Uranus again suggests a rather compulsive issue around freedom, individual rights, democracy, and so on. I get very much of the feeling of the workers' beautifully organised utopia with Uranus in the sixth. Saturn-Uranus will certainly attempt to create a society which operates according to an impeccably organised, carefully thought pattern of equality and sharing. Or at least it will pretend to do so, but the Saturn-Neptune conjunction in the twelfth suggests something else at work beneath the surface, which is not in the least inclined to equality and sharing.

As if these two Saturnian contacts weren't difficult enough, the sun in Scorpio, and Mercury, are in square to all three. So there is a fixed T-cross at work in this chart. The sun-Saturn square is one which I've already mentioned in relation to the American chart. The same deep underlying insecurities afflict both nations. In an individual's chart there is usually an issue with the father when the sun is in square to Saturn. Often there is no father, or there is a feeling of the relationship having failed, so that the person is forever fighting authority in the world yet longing for it at the same time. I don't think it's unreasonable to suggest that the issue of a lack of strong paternal models is a problem for both Russia and America. America has never had a ruling family, with a king who could stand in as father, and Russia murdered its royal family and killed the father and his heritage. There is a terrific sense of alienation when the contact with the father is lost. Many more politically left-wing orientated people in England snipe at the royal family, but it stands as a very potent archetypal image of stability and continuity. There is a different feeling with a country where no such figurehead is present to take the unconscious projection of parental authority and strength.

Another characteristic of sun-Saturn is its slight colouration of paranoia, I think in part because of the same issue of feeling no sense of continuity. There is a feeling that no one will provide support, they must always do it themselves. This produces a marvellous self-sufficiency, but it's also very difficult for relationships with others because one can never receive anything comfortably without suspicion of dependency. There is often a great overcompensation, and a touchiness about receiving help or gifts of any kind. You can see these patterns to a greater or lesser extent in any sun-Saturn configuration in an individual chart. I think the same applies to the country. You can see a little of why when America and Russia get together to talk about reducing nuclear armaments and learning to trust each other, it eventually goes sour. Both national charts have the sun-Saturn, and neither is able to trust anyone at all.

You can, I hope, begin to get a feeling of the national psyche from this configuration of sun, Saturn, Neptune, Uranus, Mercury. Tremendous idealism has to sit side by side with a religious fervour that the political ideology denies, and the need for absolute control and autocracy has to jostle with a genuine belief in individual freedom. If this were a person, I would send him into analysis immediately. Russia copes with the terrific tension and pressure by invading other countries and operating a police state under the guise of a free society, where people are forever trying to escape and disappear, and where it is necessary to censor all communication that might reveal the truth. This is very sad, because the dream of Uranus and Neptune is probably very real in the national psyche. The autocratic quality of Saturn in Leo wages internal war against the liberal ideology of Uranus, and both of them undermine the stable sense of identity which the sun represents.

The transits across this chart reveal the aliveness of national horoscopes. Each time Saturn has passed across the natal sun, the Russian leader has died or been removed from office. This is the case when Stalin took over from Lenin, when Kruschchev took over from Stalin, and when Brezhnev took over from Kruschchev. Brezhnev is of course due soon, because Saturn will be in Scorpio in a very few years' time. That's not a startling prediction, because he's getting a little shaky in his old age. If Saturn is approaching the sun by transit in an individual's chart, the year preceding the exact transit is usually fraught with a lot of soul-searching and the death of old attitudes and values which were once dominant. In an inner sense, the old king dies and there is a period of confusion and sometimes depression before new values emerge. What has happened in Russia is that just preceding the transit, the old leader dies or is deposed, and there is a power struggle which goes on until someone emerges at the top. The country of course cannot vote for its ruler as it might in a democratic system, so there's no chance for the soul-searching and reflection to take place.

What hasn't happened to Russia is the approaching transit of Pluto through Scorpio. The present political entity is too young to have experienced this transit before. I will be very curious indeed to see what comes of it. If Saturn brings down the head of the government, what will Pluto do? Perhaps the entire structure will change. Pluto always brings profound changes and rids a person of things which he has outgrown. It's a kind of fate. If the person can't meet the challenge to change, then he breaks down. That is very likely to happen in Russia, because there isn't a great deal of inclination shown to alter the system in any way except to tighten it. The conjunction of Saturn, Uranus and Neptune in Capricorn which we have approaching toward the end of this decade will conjunct Russia's natal Venus in Capricorn in the fifth house, and oppose natal Pluto in the eleventh. This happens at roughly the same time that Pluto hits the natal sun. Now in an individual's chart Venus deals with relationships and partnerships, and transits like this would put enormous pressure on that side of life. You often see marriages breaking down when the outer planets transit over Venus. Russia is a conglomerate of many different nations, not all of whom went into the marriage very willingly. Poland and Czechoslavakia and Hungary may be thinking of divorce. I would understand those transits in part to mean that there is some kind of severing of the interconnecting countries that make up the Soviet Union, which of course they could only do if the central government were to collapse. Otherwise they would simply be trampled again, as they have been in the past. Put simplistically I would say that there will be a tremendous eruption from the collective, perhaps the beginnings of an internal revolution, happening at the same time that the central authority is not in a position to prevent it. Then there would be a period of disintegration, and a potential for a new birth. If this were an individual, he could seek help of various kinds to retain some ego continuity while the changes were happening. But a country can't get help of that kind. And a sun-Saturn country wouldn't ask for

it anyway. So it may be that Pluto takes on the very literal meaning of death, and the Union of Soviet Socialist Republics will no
longer be a union.

I think that these national charts are representative of a kind
of specific incarnation for the soul of a people. You can't really
tell anything about the qualities of the soul, any more than you
can determine the qualities of a human soul from the birth chart.
This particular mundane chart is a terribly difficult one, I think by
far the most difficult of the ones we have looked at so far. The
nature of the aspects and the houses in which the planets are
placed suggest a breakdown of some kind as an inherent potential
from the outset. The tension is too great. An individual might
handle it and create from it. But countries are more fated.

Audience: Russia tried to set up a father figure in Stalin, but in
the end it didn't last. They had to pull him down.

Liz: Yes, I suppose that's why he was permitted to get away with
what he did. The need for a strong paternal figure was so great.
The czars were called "Little Father," which I think is interesting
as well. Stalin had the sun in Capricorn, so he presented a good
hook for the collective's paternal projections. In a sense what we
are dealing with here might be considered a mythic theme which
runs through the history of the Russian psyche. At least this
theme has been present since the founding of Russia as we know
it. The aspect of sun and Saturn deals with conflicts around the
father, and that is a mythic theme. An individual's life is inter-
sected by mythic themes, and some of these can be seen through
the sign emphasis and the aspects. The quarrel between the old
king and his son is symbolised in part by the quarrel between the
sun and Saturn. Here we have a nation who is also embodying the
mythic relationship between the old king and his son.

You cannot of course take a horoscope and flatly declare that
a person's "myth" in the sense that Jung means it is so-and-so
based on the horoscope. You can only get inferences of particular
dramas that are likely to repeat and repeat during the course of
life on many different levels. One of the dramas or themes which
I associate with sun-Saturn is the loss of the father, and the search
to find him in some form, and the perpetual dissatisfaction and
anger which emerge when he is found. At the same time that the
father must be overthrown, he is also sought. I think that Russia

is perpetually seeking these father-figures, but when they have ruled for a while they are experienced as terribly repressive, and then they must be rejected and a new one found. The father inevitably fails with sun-Saturn, because ultimately any father "outside" is not the object of the quest. It's an internal ordering principle that is sought. It may sound bizarre to you, but in a way Soviet Russia would do much better to restore their old royal lines. Of course they can't, but sun-Saturn is a lot like sun in Capricorn with its love of hierarchy and tradition. But with the square, it takes immense effort to acknowledge this, because one fights a square.

With an individual who has a configuration such as this T-cross in the Russian chart, you can help as an astrologer by putting the person in touch with the mythic themes which form the backdrop of his experiences. This is a connection which Jung felt to be very important, because if it happens in depth, rather than merely as an intellectual theory, it gives dignity and insight into what otherwise seem really petty and pathetic problems. A myth reflects an archetypal pattern, and that can help a person to understand that there are things at work in his psyche and his life beyond his sickness and trouble. It should also be possible to do this with a nation, but that would take a very enlightened ruler. In a sense this is a religious function, this connecting of ordinary life and myth. It's really the role of the priest, who helps an individual get in touch with his gods. With some knowledge of depth psychology it might be possible to reintroduce a nation to its lost myths.

It's interesting to look at the Russian chart from the point of view of what myths are alive in it, and what might be offered to its people along the lines of the myth. Russia has been very interested in parapsychology and the unknown aspects of the mind for a long time, but this is primarily from a scientific and not a mythic point of view. Concern with unseen matters is characteristic of Scorpio, but a rigidly materialistic approach to them is not. Perhaps that's a reflection of the sun-Uranus square, but the square between sun and Neptune requires something more mystical, perhaps more freedom for the orthodox rituals of the church. There has always been a deep mystical feeling in the Russian people, but it isn't permitted expression now.

I think it's worth considering now the conjunction which is approaching toward the end of the decade, because the Russian chart of all the national charts we have looked at is most strongly affected by it. So I would think that this country is certainly one which will react powerfully to the conjunction. The conjunction consists of first Saturn and Uranus in Sagittarius at the end of 1986. This goes on through 1987 and then finally in February 1988 Saturn and Uranus move into Capricorn and begin to conjunct Neptune. In June of that year Saturn and Uranus move retrograde back into Sagittarius for a while, and then at the end of the year they are all lined up in Capricorn again. This continues through February 1990. Then Saturn moves out of orb of the Uranus-Neptune conjunction which continues through the winter of 1997.

When Saturn gets mixed up with the outer planets, one of the results is that things exteriorise themselves in concrete terms in the world. I would therefore expect that, although the conjunction represents many other things on a deeper level, one of its effects is to produce concrete changes in Russia. There is a tendency at the moment for many astrologers and psychics to think in terms of holocausts and tidal waves and atomic destruction and the earth leapfrogging on its polar axis. But the core of an outer planet conjunction is, as we have seen with the Uranus-Neptune conjunction that occurred at the time of Marx's birth, a change in the values and needs of the collective. It doesn't inherently mean disaster. The people who are born under that conjunction will reach adulthood in the new millennium, and they will no doubt manifest in their lives the vision which the conjunction reflects. I am not saying that there will be no problems of a political or economic kind. But I would be surprised if the world ended. It's very possible that the Russian regime may topple, but, depending on your point of view, that could be seen as the beginning of a new world rather than the end of one. Certainly that would be the feeling of nations like Hungary and Czechoslavakia and Poland.

I would like to spend a bit of time analysing this conjunction. We've already met with its components, Uranus and Neptune. Briefly, this suggests a new social or political vision emerging out of the collective, coupled with a mystical or religious yearning. But the coming conjunction falls in Capricorn, whereas when Marx was born it was in Sagittarius. So the realm of life which is contained in the vision is different. We must first ask what spheres of life are represented by Capricorn. I think one of Capricorn's connections is the principle of government. Capricorn is also concerned with social hierarchy. I think the sign has much deeper and subtler levels, which are reflected by the old Renaissance idea that Saturn ruled the world of the occult and the initiate as well as the world of substance. Capricorn is also symbolic of the soul's imprisonment in physical reality, and the typical Capricornian depression is very bound up with the feeling that the world is a place of bondage, to the body, to responsibilities, to law, to conscience, to God. There are characteristic moods in Capricorn, and they are often about isolation, separateness, and self-sufficiency. Capricorn crystallises and structures and concretises. The valuing of tradition and the forms of the past also belong to the sign. I am sure there are many more things I could mention, but these are some of the main themes. I suppose I would encapsulate it by saying that the mastery of the world by the ego is Capricorn's intent, just as the striving for goodness and wisdom to fulfill the divine intent is at the core of Sagittarius.

Marx and his generation changed the religious bedrock on which human ethical codes were based, by postulating that the real dominant in life was property, not God. Now we have a similar kind of change or reversal about to happen in connection with Capricorn's meaning. Of course we can only speculate, and not speculate very well, because any genuine change by the outer planets can't be anticipated or it wouldn't really be a change. It would just be an alteration or an extension. You can only comprehend what you are able to comprehend through the quality of your ego consciousness, and if that is changing then the change is into the unknown. But at least we can try a few intuitive hunches.

I think the conviction that material reality is the only reality is a typically Capricornian vision, and all of the strivings and ethics and behaviour patterns of Capricorn stem from this view of the nature of reality. It's possible that this central attitude, in which we are all born and develop, may change. It's almost impossible to imagine what that would be like, because we have in our lifetimes never seen things differently. Certainly our ideas of government and of who is a suitable leader are built upon the same world-view. This was not always the case, and I think it's part of the reason why we find it so difficult now to really understand the medieval mind, or the mind of the ancient Greek where the world teemed with gods. The isolation and defensiveness of Capricorn stems from this same identification with not only material reality, but with the power and effectiveness of the ego. I don't think it would be too farfetched to envision changes through scientific research which offer us a completely different view not only of the physical universe but of the nature of the human being.

Now this conjunction transits across Russia's natal Venus and comes into opposition with the natal Pluto, and this occurs during the same period that transiting Pluto moves across Russia's natal sun. Because Venus concerns partnership arrangements, which in terms of countries translates into allies and satellite nations, I would expect the Union of Soviet Socialist Republics to become something other than a union. Venus-Pluto has a way of trying to coerce partners, because the problem of power enters into relationships, and this is precisely what Russia has done. These forced marriages may explode. If the central government is in a state of chaos and change through the transit of Pluto, and a new vision of reality begins to seep its way into the collective which undermines the present material ethic, then it wouldn't be surprising to see a revolution within the country. The innate religious spirit in the Russian people has been imprisoned and repressed, and it would very likely break through if it were given half a chance.

If an individual were challenged in this way, he might go through a very turbulent time, and perhaps have a breakdown of some kind, so that the rigidity of the ego's viewpoint could alter and become more flexible and inclusive of new attitudes. This might coincide with the breakup of a marriage, and a time of depression and isolation and gradual reorientation. But the Russian government does not have the flexibility of an individual psyche. If Russia breaks down, a completely different form of rulership will become necessary. There is no room for movement in this country's system, as there might be for example in England with her diversity of political parties. So it can only break down.

Audience: Perhaps there will be a return to a feudal system.

Liz: I don't think it's possible to go backward once the collective has moved beyond a particular phase. A country can break down and disintegrate and fall into chaos, but something new will always emerge. The feudal system was built upon a society where there was no concept or experience of individuality. You were a king, a prince, a knight, a merchant, a priest or a serf. The experience of individual worth and value is I think here to stay. Feudalism could never work in a world where individual consciousness has developed to the extent it has. In very backward nations it might still be operable, but I don't think that's the case with Russia.

On the other hand the tradition of kingship, seen in a new light, might not be impossible. The mystical view of kingship is that he rules but does not govern. He is a symbol of God on earth, but not a tyrant or a dictator. The psychological importance of a royal family is that they carry the projections of the Self for the collective. They represent the permanent, ancient thing which time cannot alter and which carries the powerful symbol of royal lineage. Of course in the modern world we are skeptical of these things. But kings and queens are one of the commonest dream motifs, and despite conscious cynicism they still carry powerful meaning for us.

So far my observations on the coming conjunction haven't turned up anything horribly destructive. I am sure that great changes are signified, but they don't have a violent feeling about them, at least not in any extraordinary sense. Capricorn is a good solid sign, and I think the fantasy of the end of the world is the way in which the unconscious portrays great changes in consciousness. It's probably worth looking at what happened the last time Saturn, Uranus and Neptune were all lined up together. When Marx was born, Saturn was not included in the conjunction. The last time in fact was in around 1307. Now I'm sure that this date is not going to make you all leap out of your seats because it isn't a very memorable date historically speaking. The conjunction occurred then in Scorpio. A few things did happen which were ultimately of great significance, but they seem small from the event point of view. The King of France at that time, Philippe le Bel, needed money. In order to get it, he decided to appropriate the vast monetary resources of the Knights Templar, the warlike religious order which kept a semi-independent political state and only answered to the Pope for its authority. But Philippe couldn't disband the Templars without getting a papal ratification, and the Pope refused. Being resourceful, he had the Pope assassinated, and bribed the college of cardinals to elect his own candidate as Pope. This new Pope still showed reluctance, so Philippe had him kidnapped and taken to France and installed at the papal palace at Avignon. This is what is known as the Babylonian Captivity.

Now apart from being an interesting piece of historical trivia, this event had vast repercussions. Medieval Europe saw the Church as the one infallible and unshakeable thing in life. Life was pretty hard and unreliable, what with plagues and lawlessness and famines and so on. The Pope was God's Vicar on Earth, much more infallible and semi-divine than we imagine him to be now. What Philippe le Bel did was throw the Church into chaos, from which it never properly recovered. For a time there were two Popes running concurrently, one in Rome and one in Avignon. Each thought the other one was the Antichrist. It was said that during the time of the Babylonian Captivity, no one was saved. The total faith in the Church was seriously rocked, and no sooner did it begin to attempt a recovery than the Reformation started. So the year 1307 marked the beginning of the end of the absolute power of the Church, the one voice which declared the nature and meaning of reality for the whole of the known world.

I think this little historical vignette is very instructive for us now, because I understand this conjunction to mean that some basic interpretation of reality which we have taken for granted for a long time and which holds absolute authority for us will begin to be shaken. I don't know what that could be. One can only speculate. The previous conjunction which I mentioned occurred in Scorpio, and one might think in terms of the issues that Scorpio deals with. The nature of good and evil and the conflict between them, the duality of man as beast and spiritual being, the nature of power, are all Scorpionic issues. The core of the medieval Church rested on the idea that man was a creature of sin, fallen from grace because of Adam's error, steeped in carnal desires and bestiality, and that the One True Church could save him from damnation. The means of enforcing these beliefs were fairly Scorpionic too, such as torture and severe penances. One can make a case for the great change occurring in man's view of God and the Devil.

I keep going back to the issues with which Capricorn is concerned, and each time I think about it I come up with the material view of reality. By this I don't mean materialism as a financial or economic viewpoint. A Marxist would probably hope that this was the case, but frankly I don't think money is really a Capricornian problem. But seeing the world only through the senses is, and my own subjective feeling about this conjunction is that it will affect our assumptions about the nature of the physical universe and the human body. I don't interpret this as a great millenarian explosion, for all the reasons which I have just talked about. I don't doubt that many things will change and perhaps become rather difficult in a material sense, because the world is getting itself into trouble with its energy resources and there are many problems connected with distribution of wealth. But I have yet to be convinced that this conjunction heralds the Third World War. The European Economic Community might become a United States of Europe, and you might have to run your car on chicken droppings, but I somehow expect that the world will still be here by the year 2000. I fancy that I can already see the direction this all might go in, because of the new discoveries which are being made about the apparent intelligence and interconnectedness of what we previously thought was inanimate matter. But I suppose like everybody else I will have to just wait and be surprised.

Audience: Could we be confronted with the end of the belief that a good life depends on technology and the whole materialistic-industrial idea?

Liz: I have no idea. I suspect that these kinds of hopes and questions stem from one's own personal political viewpoint, but the outer planets bring changes that can't really be envisaged because we have never experienced them before. The question you have raised isn't a new one. People have been complaining about that since the Cretans invented a flushing toilet. I think it's something more profound than that. I would suggest you read Norman Cohn's book, *The Pursuit of the Millenium.* The fantasy that the destruction of evil technology and machines will lead back to the golden age where no one quarrelled about property is an archetypal fantasy. It was around in the Middle Ages very strongly. All this means is that we are projecting our own evil onto machines. That doesn't accomplish a lot. Technology has made our lives enormously fruitful, and given us a chance to develop inwardly. Technology is the outward reflection of differentiated ego consciousness. If an individual projects all his values into his gadgets, that is his problem, not the inherent evil of the gadget. The medieval millenarian cults had the same idea about medieval technology. The devil was in material things, because it's much harder to look at the devil in yourself. Besides, I don't think Capricorn is concerned with technology. That is much more Aquarian and in line with Aquarius' vision of man's intellect gaining mastery over nature by stealing her secrets.

Pluto is transiting through Scorpio while this conjunction is moving through Capricorn. I mentioned some things earlier about Pluto in Scorpio, and how this transit of the planet through its own sign seems to resurrect ancient views which have been dead for a long time and which deal with the nature of the soul, immortality and rebirth. I find this combination of transits exciting rather than terrifying. In a worldly sense I am sure Russia will be strongly affected, but that doesn't disturb me because I do not have great sympathy for the human imprisonment which occurs under that political system. Apart from this, I have no clear idea of mundane changes. I think it's possible to become very stupid, and because of the tension which deep collective changes generate, run around trying to blame one political system or another for all the world's woes. But I suspect that it's wiser to be pragmatic and wait, because the outer planets are always surprising. Because it falls in an earthy sign, the conjunction makes me feel much more that we might emerge with a better understanding of the physical world we live in, rather than being blown up. But of course I can be accused of being an optimist.

The conjunction affects the charts of other nations as well, and one of them is England. Whether you take the chart for the crowning of William the Conqueror or the chart for the founding of the United Kingdom, the sun is in Capricorn and will be transited by the conjunction. Likewise America will be affected by the conjunction, because it falls in opposition to America's sun, Venus and Jupiter in Cancer. I think this time that I will leave you all to speculate on what it all might mean.

The sphere of religion is perhaps also connected to the approaching conjunction, because I think Capricorn concerns the formal side of life in general and the formal side of religion in particular. The religious spirit is not necessarily reflected by Saturn, but the dogma of religion is, because it is the formal container in which the mystical vision is enclosed. Religious dogma is an effort to recreate a mystery which occurred once, whether that is embodied in Moses receiving the Tablets of the Law or the birth of Jesus or the revelation of Mohammed or the enlightenment of the Buddha. Form is in this sense an effort at making continuous and eternal something which is by its nature momentary and miraculous. I feel that the formal issues of religion are very important to many Capricorns, and much of the sign's journey involves loss of faith, despair, finding of faith and humility. We associate the knees with Capricorn, and the knees are what we kneel on when we make obeisance.

I have noticed a peculiarity about Saturn placed in the ninth house, which of course is the house associated with religious attitudes and the person's image of God. Planets in the ninth describe what kind of God we experience, and what powers and attributes we give to the divine. Saturn in the ninth is an Old Testament god, who upholds principles such as justice, law, humility, correct behaviour, conscience, and good works. Saturn in the ninth is terribly sensitive to the formal side of religion with its codes of behaviour, which in some cases leads to the person becoming anti-religious because he can't live with the demands of his God within himself. So he rejects religion in the hope that it will take away his conscience, which is almost always horribly highly developed, and then discovers that God gets just as angry from the unconscious. The Old Testament Yahveh is a proud and jealous God, and he probably loves Job because Job is another Capricorn like himself, enduring and long-suffering and uncomplaining and as stubborn as a mule. I have the feeling that there are spheres of religious outlook which are going to be strongly affected by the conjunction, and they deal with the formal or dogmatic aspects of religion rather than the inherent beliefs. Perhaps the structure of the great religions which have existed for so many centuries will undergo some change. That's certainly a strong possibility, since there is already a great deal of unrest and dissatisfaction within the religious communities.

Audience: Could the conjunction falling on England's chart mean that England loses her sovereignty and becomes part of Europe, or something like that?

Liz: I don't know. Your speculations are as good as mine. That's certainly a possibility. There are all kinds of possibilities. The nature of England as a monarchy could change. The structure of the government, with its House of Lords and House of Commons, could change. Or it could maintain all these things and become a state in a united Europe. I really have no idea. The only thing I'm fairly certain about is that total destruction is Pluto's talent, and

Pluto is not part of this conjunction. This is change without total destruction.

Audience: I know you're leaving it up to us to speculate, but can't you do just a little speculation about the way the conjunction affects America's chart? My speculations are pretty alarming, because the seventh house is the house of enemies.

Liz: Well, there is always that possibility. I would prefer to interpret the seventh house as the house of relationships, in which both friendly terms and conflicts are experienced. I can only tell you what I would say if it were a person with the sun, Venus and Jupiter in the seventh and the conjunction of Saturn, Uranus and Neptune transited through the first house and opposed those Cancer planets. If Pluto were involved, I would expect power struggles, a bitter divorce with a lot of manipulation and difficulty, or the death of the partner, or the person realising that he can no longer tolerate the other in his life. But Pluto is not involved here. Saturn usually carries with it soul-searching confrontations with oneself, and acceptance of limitations, and loneliness. Neptune often brings disillusionment and a dream that doesn't quite work out as expected. And Uranus suggests to me separations, a parting of the ways. All these planets are moving through the first, which means that the person himself, or country itself, is the one doing the soul-searching and changing. It isn't someone outside causing it.

I think I mentioned earlier that seventh house suns are not terribly self-sufficient. They need relationships in order to develop, and they don't like being alone for very long. There is a tendency to get bound up in everybody else's business, and to function as a mediator. A seventh house sun can be a very creative mediator. I have seen many people with this placement in the helping professions, Jung among them, and likewise Freud. They are drawn to trying to resolve conflicts, and in the process they themselves develop and grow. I think this is typical of America. America has its hands in every country's business. It tends to promote the image of the mediator, policing the world to keep it free. Although America is insular in terms of its culture, and many Americans pride themselves on never having left their home towns, it is not in the least insular in terms of political and economic entanglements with other nations. This tendency to try to mediate is on the one hand admirable, and on the other rather unfortunate, since other countries sometimes become resentful at the interference. Also, since America's sun is in square to Saturn in the tenth, there is the unpleasant hard reality of its own government sometimes meeting a somewhat lower standard than the one which America demands that its fellow countries meet. In short, the sun-Saturn square has a touch of self-undoing about it. The very noble ideals of the seventh house collide with the embarrassment of internal politics.

The issue of America's entanglements with other countries is the thing which I think is affected by the transit. Whether the trigger is, for example, the Arab nations refusing to supply oil, or whatever, it looks to me like a period of national soul-searching and tightening of belts. I think there will be a severing of dependencies, which will come as a great shock to the people because there is so much of an illusion of self-sufficiency. The resources for self-sufficiency are of course there, but they haven't been properly tapped. In an individual's chart, this kind of transit suggests that the sense of identity is being given a good working-over. America's identity is much too bound up with how the rest of the world sees it. Venus and Jupiter together in the seventh suggest a kind of extravagance, not only materially, but in terms of the sense of self-importance. I think this is likely to be a marvellously creative transit, because it's a kind of growing up. I don't intend to offend the Americans in the group, and I don't mean all this in a nastily critical way. But America, unlike the European countries, is a very young nation with tremendous vitality which has never been invaded or conquered or forced into submission, and which has never had to undergo the centuries of grinding struggle and poverty that have afflicted Europe. The 1929 depression was a ghastly shock to America, because such a thing had never been experienced before. But every country in Europe has a long history of terrible deprivation, war, invasion and chaos. When I say that I think the transit is a growing-up time, it isn't meant as an insult, but as a statement of how things might actually be.

As the conjunction moves into the latter part of Capricorn, Saturn moves ahead and is no longer involved. Uranus and Neptune then move across America's second house Pluto. This house deals with the resources and wealth both of a country and of an individual. Because Saturn isn't involved, I would say that this might concern changes in values. The American emphasis on material wealth and expansion is perhaps going to undergo quite a change. Pluto in the second house is a very acquisitive position, and tends to be intense and passionate about its wealth, but it also tends to undergo radical changes at long intervals. In mundane astrology Pluto is said to rule monopolies and huge conglomerates of companies, because of the issue of power involved. So I would say that there is a good possibility of major changes in this sphere. You can certainly piece together a scenario out of this. Of course it might not be the right scenario. But it's the way I am inclining, rather than envisioning war with Russia.

I think in the end it's equally productive to consider this conjunction in terms of what it does to your own chart. That's perhaps more edifying because we can only talk about countries in terms of generalities, whereas an individual knows the pattern of his own life much more intimately. Besides, he has some say in what happens to him individually, much more than he does about his country. I know how easy it is to become alarmed about outer planet transits, because they are beyond the individual's scope and control. But if they bring changes which are difficult or unpleasant, we all have some say about how we are going to respond to those changes. I think that what Jung says is very relevant—that an individual's life is characteristic of himself. What comes into your life is needed and is an opportunity. I think this is particularly true of the outer planets, which frighten the ego but open it up so that the person can live more of what he potentially needs to become.

Audience: Can you say anything about earthquakes? A number of astrologers feel that the conjunction will set off a giant earthquake in California.

Liz: I have no idea. There have been expectations of a giant earthquake for a long time. I think one would have to look at California's chart, which I haven't got. A state has a chart just as a nation does. If the entire state were going to drop off into the Pacific Ocean, then I think the conjunction would have to be hitting something pretty powerfully in California's birth chart. I really can't speculate about earthquakes. There are a number of clairvoyant prophecies about this, but I am always suspicious because clairvoyant visions are like dreams, they often symbolise something rather than stating a literal fact. One could make a case for this because California's oil is critical to America's economy; and if there were a massive disaster, then it would hit America's pocketbook very hard, which might be indicated by the transiting conjunction moving across the second house Pluto. I really don't know. I have personally always feared a major earthquake in California, but that's more to do with my own fantasies than with any astrological prognostication. An earthquake is a very primordial symbol of destruction. It's an act of God, which is what insurance policies call it. There is obviously room for some research here. But I would want to see California's chart before I really began to speculate.

Audience: What part of the chart would you look at?

Liz: The ascendant, because it's the entity itself, the corporeal form. The ascendant in an individual's chart is the point of his incarnation. So it traditionally rules the physical body, and the basic outlook toward life. I think the same applies to the ascendant of a state or city or country. The tenth house represents the style of government, just as the tenth house in the person's chart represents his conscious social values and codes of behaviour. We like to be seen as our midheavens, but what we truly are in essence is much more the ascendant and the sun. The second house is the entity's resources, and so on. If a person has a strong transit through the tenth house, then he will often change jobs, or alter his career goals, or present himself in a completely different way to the world. But a strong transit over the ascendant changes your basic character. Or maybe I should say that it reveals more of your basic character than you had previously been aware of.

I will repeat for the third time that I'm not an expert on mundane astrology. You might read Charles Carter's book on political astrology, which is very good, but there are very few books in print at the moment where any new light has been shed on this area of astrology. Once upon a time it was terribly important to study the charts of nations and cities. I found a book recently in the British Museum Library which dates from the sixteenth century, which is a sort of Renaissance version of Margaret Hone. It's a huge three-volume text for the student of astrology, unfortunately written in Latin. Most of the instructions are devoted to the interpretation of judicial charts, the charts of cities and nations. There are a handful of birth horoscopes of the individual notables of the time, various kings and princes and dukes. But the main emphasis is on mundane charts. The author was a man called Luc Gauricus, who was astrologer to several ruling Italian families. He wouldn't have dreamt of doing his work without having to hand the birth horoscopes for the cities of Florence, Venice, Mantua, and so on. Otherwise how could he have told his patrons what was going to happen to them? We have lost all this now. I'm quite ignorant of the really subtle principles of mundane astrology, and I think someone will eventually have to translate Luc Gauricus' work into English so that we can relearn what was once an honoured aspect of astrological study.

There was of course no psychological interpretation of the chart in the sixteenth century, because there was no concept of a psyche. Plato and other Greek philosophers had a lot to say about the psyche, but the mainstream of astrology parted ways with Plato some time before Luc Gauricus. So all the individuals and countries that Gauricus writes about are fated. There is no such thing as choice. King Henri II of France will die in his forty-first year in a joust through a wound in the eye. As it turns out, Gauricus was quite accurate about that one. King Henri died precisely on time as predicted. It would never have occurred to either Gauricus or King Henri, who knew about the prophecy, that there was any way out. There was no concept of internalising a problem. But the principles of mundane astrology have perhaps not changed so much. I think that nations are a little less fated than they were because people in general are a little more conscious and much of the world is freer and can at least make a show of electing or removing its rulers. But maybe that's unduly optimistic, because Nazi Germany was only forty years ago, and Khomeini's Iran is not so very different from a fourteenth-century Italian city-state with a tyrannical ruler.

Audience: How would you set up a chart for a country with no particular founding, such as Wales?

Liz: You can't. You would have to use the chart for the United Kingdom, but as any Welshman could tell you, Wales has its own identity. But there are nations which exist as psychically independent entities yet which are not separate countries in a political sense. In a literal sense, Wales is not a separate country. Whether that's right or wrong I leave to the Welsh to debate.

Audience: Perhaps you could work with the chart of a national hero, such as Owen Glendower.

Liz: That's certainly a possibility, if you could get Owen Glendower's chart. But I'm afraid it's about as accessible as Jesus Christ's chart. Owen Glendower is a myth as well as an actual man, and he certainly embodies the free spirit of Wales. But there is no birth data on him. The best you could do with Wales would be to work with individual Welsh towns and cities, each of which will have a charter for its birth as an entity. I'm afraid there isn't much else you can do.

The same problem exists with Scotland. I think many parts of modern nations feel they are really not the same as the main political body, yet their birth data is impossible to obtain. Or you can find a people such as the Basques who try to fight violently for their autonomy. The duchy of Lorraine has always resented being part of France. The American South of course fell into civil war in an effort to establish its own autonomy. All the satellite nations of the Soviet Union have their original identities such as Latvia and Lithuania and so on. But we can't do charts for them. At least not yet.

It may sound terribly unfair if you are very patriotic about Wales or Scotland or Lithuania, but as I said before, these mundane horoscopes are political entities, not the souls of peoples. Wales is not a separate country. I don't mean to offend the Welsh, but it is part of the United Kingdom, which has a birth chart. England is easy, because of the chart for the crowning of William the Conqueror. But the problem arises again with Germany. Modern West Germany is hardly representative of the German people in a historical sense. Germany was never united until Bismarck's time. Bavaria was a separate kingdom and so was Prussia. There were individual duchies and states loosely bound under the umbrella of the old Habsburg Holy Roman Empire. All you can do is throw up your hands and resign yourself to the horoscope for West Germany which was born after the last war.

There is a mystical tradition that different nations are ruled by different signs in a soul sense. That is, the true national character is reflected by a particular sign, regardless of what political entity has been foisted on that national soul at any time in history. That's an attractive idea, but of course one can't work with it practically. I can imagine that Russia might be a Scorpio or Germany might be an Aries or whatever, but I can never know whether that's my own projection on that nation. So we'll leave that side of it out. It's a bit like trying to get a chart for the individual Self, which is what Alice Bailey writes about. It's wonderful stuff, and very inspiring, but you can't do anything with it in a practical sense. It's all very well to believe that you respond to the Seventh Ray and that your soul is really a Virgo. But in the end you're stuck with the horoscope for your birth, because in the end that's the life you've got to live. I hope I haven't depressed any Welshmen. But I don't suppose I have, because my impression is that they have a pretty clear sense of the soul.

Lecture Six

Several people have asked questions about individual configurations in their own charts involving the outer planets, and I think it would be a good idea to spend some time discussing these points. One query made to me earlier was about the effect of the Jupiter-Saturn conjunction over a fifth house sun and Neptune. I would say very briefly that this is probably about the opening up of creative channels. The sun in the fifth house is not automatically self-expressive and spontaneous and creative. There is always a struggle with the sun, and it doesn't get moving until the thirties. And Neptune, which brings the mystical, imaginal world into focus, suggests to me that in order to develop your own sense of individuality you will have to let go long enough to allow the nonrational realm to touch you. I get the feeling of someone who desperately needs to let the world of dreams and fantasies and moods and irrational feeling states up into consciousness, because until you can do that you'll never feel like an individual. I think Jupiter might trigger the eruption of that world, while Saturn demands that you find an outlet for it other than emotional hysteria or wild fantasies of what you might do one day.

Audience: That's very interesting, because it's crossed my sun once already and I felt I was coming unglued. It was a very revealing experience, but I was getting worried about what would happen when it crossed the second time.

Liz: Nothing is going to happen that's particularly different from what's already started to happen. You might see different facets of a basic problem. When a planet makes a retrograde passage over a particular point in the chart, it's a bit like successive chapters in the same book. Different action occurs, but the same theme runs all the way through. Events may differ, but the underlying meaning is the gradual unfoldment into consciousness of whatever the birth planet represents. I have noticed that the first transit often opens up a new area—something new is discovered, either outside or inside oneself. The retrograde passage on the second round is a kind of consolidation and effort to understand what it is that has been happening. But there is often a blocked or unresolved feeling with that retrograde passage. One can't do anything yet with the insights. Then the third chapter comes when the planet moves across going direct, and there is usually some kind of breakthrough or external change which allows you to make use of what you have learned. Events may surprise you, but the underlying theme will be the same.

Audience: I've got the sun, moon and Jupiter in Taurus and Mercury in Gemini. I don't know much about it. I wonder if you'd care to comment.

Liz: I wouldn't really. I think this is part of basic interpretation, and I don't want to get tied up doing that since I would like to keep to the main theme of the collective. Perhaps someone else would like to say something.

Audience: Well, I have Mercury in Gemini like this lady, and it tends to make me very talkative.

Liz: Perhaps you can talk to each other. I think that if Mercury is in a sign different from the sun-sign, what the individual says and what is really motivating him are often very different. Perhaps that applies to you. Mercury in Gemini is very quick and fluid and versatile. It can come up with quick answers and get a quick, clear picture. Taurus is a much slower sign, and the deeper values are much earthier. I think your head runs much faster than the rest of you. It may take you a while to work out what you really want.

Audience: Can I ask you about Venus-Pluto? I have them conjuncting in the tenth house.

Liz: I think I said a bit about Venus-Pluto earlier. Venus governs one's ideals and values in relationships. I think that having Pluto with it suggests that you are meant to develop those values on a deeper level than the ordinary social definitions allow. Pluto forces a person to confront the unconscious side of a relationship, which is both enriching and terrifying. If you build a relationship around that kind of honesty, then you'll be able to make it work. But if you try to cling to a more superficial way of interpreting love, then the relationship will probably break up. There isn't a bad fate around Venus-Pluto. But I think there are issues which most of us don't want to deal with, such as the inevitable hate and power struggle that runs along side by side with intense love. Also the irreconcilable dilemmas between male and female become apparent with Venus-Pluto. These things must be incorporated within the relationship. If you and your partner hide behind the newspaper each morning and pretend that everything is lovely and never quarrel, you're asking for trouble if you have Venus-Pluto. The fact that this Venus-Pluto falls in your tenth house suggests to me that both very intense passions and power orientation are qualities which you associate with your mother. For that reason you might try to disidentify from them, rather than living them in yourself. So I would say that there is also an issue with the mother, which may make it difficult for you to allow that deeper level of relationship to come into your life. That would eventually need to be faced.

Audience: I would like to ask a question on synastry involving Pluto. I have Saturn in my twelfth house, and it conjuncts my partner's Pluto which is in her twelfth house.

Liz: Yes, that's fine, because I wanted to talk about the outer planets in synastry anyway. I think you must first think about the map I put up on the board of the mountains. Powerful urges and images come up from the depths and they are stopped at the barrier of the ego by Saturn. Where Pluto is concerned, the urges are those of the uncivilised, primordial man. In an individual's chart where Saturn and Pluto are conjuncting, those primitive desires and emotions will frighten the individual, and he's likely to try to control them. Eventually they will break through the barrier, and the worse the control that has been imposed on them, the worse the impact. There is a furiously controlled feeling about Saturn-Pluto people unless they are willing to take the challenge of accepting and integrating that wild, raging, passionate instinctual creature that is the core of their animal self. So you must apply this same principle when the contact occurs between two charts.

I immediately sense a power struggle which will occur, and that isn't necessarily a bad thing if you are both conscious of it. Pluto will try to break down the defenses of Saturn, usually through emotional or sexual channels. Saturn in turn will try to control and limit Pluto, because there is a fear of the intensity that might erupt into the relationship. Sometimes you see this through heavy atmospheres, where Pluto really works on Saturn through black moods and scenes and difficult silences. Eventually I think Pluto wins this contest, if winning is the word, because Pluto is a collective planet and represents a vital need of all men and women, not just the individual's personal feelings. Saturn fears Pluto's power. Saturn's typical defenses are hyper-rationality, coldness, criticism, rejection and a sort of wet-blanket atmosphere that spoils everything for the other person. In the long term, Pluto gradually erodes some of Saturn's rigidity and Saturn helps to civilise Pluto. I don't think it's a bad combination. But I think there must be a lot of honesty, both self-honesty and honesty with the other person. Pluto carries the projection of the Dark Mother, and as this is a woman on whom you are likely to hook this archetypal image, you are likely to be very afraid of the power of her sexuality and her feelings. I think you will have to try to separate the archetypal image from the actual woman, who is probably not the witch you imagine her to be in your fantasies.

What makes aspects like this so difficult is the reluctance which people feel about working with them. I think there is a nakedness required in relationships with these combinations, and the defensiveness makes us try on all kinds of false pride and manipulation and dirty tricks in order to prevent the partner from seeing our fear and our need. Pluto is particularly embarrassing because most of us like to imagine that we are gentle, civilised people who don't have these savage, unrelenting emotions in us. But I suspect that cross-aspects like this can be a marvellous gift, if one can meet the challenge. Relationships like this force us to deepen and grow. If you just want things easy and comfortable and don't like your person threatened, you should stay away. You can't treat a relationship like this in a conventional way, hoping that everything will stay quiet and comfortable at home while you get on with bigger and better things. But the fact that you've got embroiled in it suggests to me that you want something deeper, so you have the thing you need.

I think contacts like these can be very painful and ugly at times. There can also be unpleasant endings and separations. But the opposite is also true, and the profound sense of intimacy and companionship is far greater and more enduring than the box-like shape which a more superficially inclined person makes for his relationships. If you can go your own way in terms of relationship values, and not rely on the collective model, then you're fine with aspects like this. But you must get out of your head the conventional idea of a normal relationship.

Audience: Could you comment on Pluto in the midheaven?

Liz: Yes, I should say something about the outer planets in general when they're found in the midheaven. First let's consider the MC-IC axis itself. The MC or midheaven is first of all the inheritance from the mother. It's what has come down to you from the maternal line, and it must be concretised in the world. Mother among other things is a symbol of form, of matter and material reality. She is the body out of which we come. So mother and world are bound up with each other, and the inheritance from the mother is also bound up with the vocation in life. This point in the chart isn't about one's job. It's about vocation or calling, the ideals which we seek to actualise in the world. One of the things I've noticed about outer planets in the midheaven is that it's very difficult to be satisfied with an ordinary job. One must feel that he is working for and with the collective in some way. So often it takes a long time before the person finds work which really suits him and gives him a sense of purpose. The outer planets are a pretty powerful psychic inheritance from Mother, and she is often terribly powerful and threatening because there is some very powerful urge or dynamism in her that cannot be expressed and which the child must concretise.

Now Pluto is concerned in part with the dark side of human nature, the depths of the unredeemed and uncivilised shadow. This is the dross which society has rejected, yet which still has tremendous vitality and potential. So Pluto in the midheaven implies that you must find work which will help you to confront and shape this darker face of life. Pluto represents power, the power of the unconscious and the instincts. There is always the problem with Pluto that the person who is meant to learn to work with power must first be the victim of power for a time. Otherwise he cannot use it responsibly. I've noticed that Pluto in the midheaven favours professions that encounter the dark, such as medicine and psychology, and also professions that deal with the darkness in society, which of course opens out into politics.

Carter and Nixon both have tenth house Plutos. The mother has enormous power when Pluto is in the tenth, and the individual often feels that he is her victim.

Audience: My tenth house Pluto doesn't make any major aspects.

Liz: Well, I think it's likely in that case that you aren't very aware of the fact that it belongs to you. An unaspected planet behaves in a very autonomous fashion. I think I mentioned this before. It often projects itself outward onto someone or something else, because the rest of the chart isn't naturally linked with it. Here it would very likely represent a terrific and rather dark power attached to the mother, which you might not realise is also something in you. And you might also project that power into society, into large organisations or government or wherever you feel there is power, and feel overwhelmed and threatened by it. But in the end you must still try to work with it. I think Pluto feels very like fate, because it's a blind, instinctual force. It isn't something one would have chosen. Perhaps if you found a field of work which really allowed you to interact with that darkness, you would be compelled and fascinated by it but would always feel that somehow it wasn't what you would have liked to do.

Outer planets in the tenth house can give many problems with ordinary employment, because the midheaven is how the world sees you, and if you are carrying Pluto around in a very unconscious way, then for no observable reason people whom you work with might feel threatened by you, or get into power battles with you. Others feel something threatening and they counterattack, but to you it might just feel like attack. Then one has the so-called problem with authority which Pluto in the tenth often displays. But it must be made conscious. It isn't really your mother.

There is a similar issue around Uranus and Neptune in the midheaven. Trying to follow an ordinary line of work brings many difficulties with it, because there is always a restless dissatisfied thing underneath that wants to be involved with the collective in some way. Other people pick this up if one is very unconscious of it, and they react to it. You can learn a lot about your tenth house by the way you are treated at work. But I think the usual textbook description of "unusual professions" is quite true. These planets in the tenth need outlets that connect up with the psychic life of the group. This is why you find so many of them in the entertainment fields such as films and music, and on the stage, and in the political arena, and in fields of research where breakthroughs are promised.

Audience: Would the same thing apply to me, with the moon conjunct Uranus in Cancer in the midheaven?

Liz: Yes, in general the same thing would apply. But Uranus is not concerned with the unredeemed shadow side of life. It's concerned with the new idea which will open up consciousness, and the new discovery which will enlighten or improve society. I have found that Uranus is very drawn to bringing new ideas to the public. It must function in a mentally alive atmosphere. And too much limitation or restriction is obviously going to cause problems. The moon is one's need for security, so this urge of yours to promote new things for others is also something you need for your emotional stability. Again traditionally, a tenth house Uranus can't work well for other people. It's the classic image of the individual who cannot bear a superior standing over him telling him what to do or think. One must be free to get one's hands on the stuff of new ideas. This kind of placement suggests all sorts of things to me—media, communications, education, anything which allows you to change the consciousness of the people you are dealing with.

The moon is the chart's anchor. It's the safe place, the place where we go for safety. If everything else is falling to bits, we run for the house where the moon is placed. So you would run into your career and your feeling of usefulness to the public. You also, in a sense, run to Mother. The moon in the tenth is a very strong emotional tie to the mother, a similarity of feeling responses. Her attitudes are also your attitudes. The rather rebellious, edgy, impulsive, inspired quality of moon-Uranus is the inheritance from the mother. It's also the difficult aspect of the relationship with the mother, the ambivalence she must have felt about being a mother at all. The need for freedom to move and share ideas is both hers and yours, although she probably wasn't able to live it. So you must in a sense live out her unlived life, and contribute something to a world larger than immediate family.

Audience: Can I change the theme of the discussion slightly? I can apply what you say to my chart, which also has Uranus in the midheaven. But I have it in square to Venus. I have a feeling that means that my ideas and innovations never come to fruition. At least that's how I feel about them.

Liz: In what house is your Venus placed?

Audience: In the ascendant.

Liz: I think that Venus-Uranus squares in general suggest a strong conflict between the need for others and the compulsion to pursue one's own vision, chasing after those wonderful ideas about how to change the world. Venus-Uranus in square can really interfere with your dealings with other people, and perhaps part of the reason why you can't follow things through is that you alienate the people you need to help you. Venus in the ascendant gives a certain quality to the personality, a very agreeable and reasonable and pleasant demeanor. It will always try to mediate and keep peace and please others. But Uranus in the midheaven is of course not in the least concerned with pleasing others. There is a great instability about it, which in part reflects the instability of the original relationship with the mother. I always get the feeling when Uranus describes the mother that she was pretty unhappy about being a mother in the first place. The instability that is reflected is both a quality of lack of commitment in her and the same lack of commitment in you.

I have a feeling that you get scared also when you come up with something because you might offend someone with it. Squares vacillate enormously. You can't follow the independent spirit because you need people to like you, but your need of people makes you angry so you break away at the critical moment. I think there is a great insecurity about Venus-Uranus aspects. One has been subjected to broken or severed relationships quite early in life, and there is a tendency to expect the same later. I think there must be a way in which you can try to live both ends of this square. Venus and Uranus aren't mutually irreconcilable. They seem that way very often, and you particularly see it in the dithering that people with this aspect do about permanent relationships. Yes I want it, no I don't. There is always the terror that someone else will take your freedom away, but it's really your own longing for relationship that interferes with the craving for perfect freedom.

Venus-Uranus is often afraid of compromising, because of the Uranian ideal of perfect truthfulness and the belief that one must be brutally honest in order to live up to the ideal. You can often hear Venus-Uranus going on about how people can't own each other and how jealousy and emotionality in relationships is an unevolved state. That's the Uranian vision. But they get tripped up terribly by their own unconscious emotional needs. Sometimes this happens because someone else gives you a hard time, and sometimes it's the repressed feelings which come up as apathy and depression and an inability to finish anything. I think one must learn to give equal value to both ends of this square. The more honest you can be about your need of other people, the easier that square will become. But if you try to be wholly Uranian, Venus will retaliate. Likewise if you try to be wholly Venusian and everyone's favourite nice person, then Uranus will unconsciously sabotage your relationships by making enemies unwittingly.

You can think of a square as two characters in a play. They are scripted to quarrel with each other, even if they don't feel like it, because that's the script. So they begin to haggle, and each side becomes very uncompromising. Uranus is desperately afraid of being human, and Venus is desperately afraid of being alone and inhuman. You can see the same dynamic with Venus in square to Pluto or Neptune. Venus wants lovely, nice, peaceful, happy relationships and Pluto insists that love is worth nothing without hate, conflict, battle and reconciliation. Or Venus wants a solid, safe, secure, physically real relationship, but Neptune insists that only the things of the spirit are of any value and sexuality is definitely not the way to find God. One must find room in one's life for both.

Audience: I have Venus in square to both Saturn and Uranus, which are in the twelfth house. Venus is in Virgo in the third. Does that mean I have three characters who are fighting instead of only two?

Liz: Yes, in a sense it does mean that. Saturn is concerned with self-protection, not with relationship. Saturn is the voice which warns us against too much vulnerability or dependency on another person. Uranus doesn't want to be tied either, but for different reasons. The ideal of freedom conflicts with the demands that arise from dealings with another. And Saturn and Uranus are of course inimical to each other in many ways, because Saturn clings to what is safe and practical and secure, while Uranus will dare anything in the name of an ideal.

I get a feeling from this kind of configuration that you would have great difficulty in deciding whether to bother about any relationships at all. If you project the Saturn-Uranus end of the square, then very likely you will be or have been hurt by some- one else who cannot give you the commitment you crave. But if you allow the conflict to be conscious and recognise that it's your own, then I think there are issues around trusting other people with your needs which are quite difficult. Sometimes I have seen this combination give a feeling of coldness, but it isn't really cold. It's terribly frightened both of being hurt and of being prevented from being an independent individual. There is a great fear of losing the other, and a reluctance to take that risk. Much of this will probably connect with childhood experi- ences, because this configuration often means that one loses a parent, either physically or psychologically, and the fear of separation runs very deep.

Saturn in the twelfth has a rather suspicious feeling about it, because Saturn defends himself from anything which might undermine the ego's position of strength, and the twelfth house exposes one to the chaos and boundlessness of the unconscious. So I would expect that you are not only afraid of intimacy be- cause of the problem of rejection and abandonment, but that you're afraid of it also because of the loss of self which happens if you let another person through the boundaries. Relationships of a deep kind threaten to unlock all that is hidden and unknown about yourself. What I can't tell from the chart is whether you act out this suspicion and reclusiveness yourself, or whether you find other people who will act it out for you. With Venus in Virgo it's likely that it's you yourself who cannot open up with others. A more effusive Venus might seem much more open and covertly push the partner into rejection.

I don't think squares have to remain completely antagonistic. We can go a long way toward some kind of reconciliation. I don't think it ever becomes perfect, and I would be surprised if you were ever one hundred per cent sure in a relationship either about your own commitment or about your partner's. But I think the more extreme reactions to aspects like this don't have to keep recurring. I think Venus-Saturn has a tendency to react badly if there is hurt or disappointment in love, with the attitude that it just isn't worth it and why bother to try again. It can get horribly gloomy and fatalistic about all future relationships being doomed to failure. This is taking the childhood wound and seeing it in the future instead of recognising that it's the past. Then one creates that future, because one never opens up. But loneliness and acceptance of separations is terribly important for someone with these aspects to go through. If one can take the limitations of other people in terms of love, and not keep looking for the parent who was lost and then being furious because the partner hasn't turned out to be perfect, then I think the way through for these aspects is the way of compassion for a basic human condition. Uranus finds it hard to accept this kind of thing, because one has such a rigid idea of how it ought to be. I think you may have to learn that other people are also frightened of being hurt, and that you can overuse your sensitivity and destroy relationships which could be very fulfilling even if they don't fulfill the fantasy.

In many ways the main difficulty with configurations such as this one which involve outer planets is that the body of collective values and standards about relationship is not a lot of use. When I use the word collective here, by the way, I don't mean the collective unconscious in the sense in which I have been describing those deep currents and movements which erupt into society. I mean social law, social standards on a conscious level which we are taught along with our ordinary education. Marriage in the eyes of the collective in this sense is something which is supposed to entail absolute commitment, and if there are problems then they must be solved within the unshakeable framework of the marriage. But Uranus finds a lot wrong with the institution of marriage as it is practised, and the idealism of this planet is not just illusion. There is a powerful urge to change or improve something which may be too rigid or outworn. Sometimes Uranus goes to ridiculous extremes, and denies the psychological differences between men and women, and the archetypal meaning of marriage as a symbol. But if you have an aspect between Venus and Uranus, you must find new values in relationship in some way. And collective standards can't really give much of a guideline. The art, I think, is to find a way to blend the new with the old, rather than totally destroy something precious in the name of a theoretical freedom.

There is the same problem with Neptune and Pluto. They pull

UR- Vö

the person into experiences for which collective standards have no explanation or acceptance. Pluto introduces us to the beast in ourselves, and we're taught that this thing has no value and must be eradicated or subdued. But when we do that too forcibly, then all the passion goes out of life. And Neptune tries to break down the conscious emphasis on the material side of things, so that a sense of the divine can be experienced in any aspect of life. Outer planets force us to find highly individual ways of coping, because they always personify the new thing which has not yet become an entrenched part of social conditioning. With Venus in aspect to Uranus, you are not only going to be exposed to a vision of love and relationship which seems contradictory to what you have been taught to expect. You're also exposed to the anarchy and chaos of Uranus, which can only see what must be shattered without recognising the things of value that must be included in the new thing.

Audience: I can't accept your equating anarchy with chaos.

Liz: Well, that's fine, but they are synonymous to me. Anarchy to me is a state of chaos. It's a rebellion against what is, without any creative means of integrating what's of value in what is, with what ought to be. This is the smashing of idols which one thinks are evil, without any sense of their value. Uranus is not concerned with feeling values, which are subtle and elusive and in contradiction to ideology. Something may be wrong in principle but right to an individual because of the irrational and inexplicable choice of the heart. Uranus must trample on the heart because otherwise it gets in the way of general principles. I feel that anarchy is the negative face of Uranus, just as sadism and exploitation are the negative edges of Pluto, and deceit and regression to infantility are the negative edges of Neptune.

The French Revolution is a good example of Uranus run amok. An altar was erected to Reason, yet this was one of the most profoundly unreasonable events in history. The ideas on which the Revolution were based were sane enough to begin with, and change was desperately needed in the face of the corruption of the ruling French monarchy. But once it got going, it was merely a bloodbath, and any sense of proportion was lost. Feeling gives us proportion, because it responds to individual situations. The French Revolution fell into anarchy, or chaos, if you like.

This is what I mean. The anarchy of Uranus in terms of relationship lies in its tendency to smash things because they aren't wholly right in principle, without attending to what might be right in feeling, that could be salvageable.

I think it's helpful today, as it was natural to the Greeks and to the astrologers of the Renaissance, to understand these outer planets as though they were gods. This is true of all the planets. If you study any ancient pantheon of deities, you find that each god has a very distinct identity and very distinct attributes. All the gods are double-faced, they have a creative pole and a destructive one. Each deity is incomplete without the others, and each has his or her excesses. There is a tremendously creative face to the outer planets, and also a terribly destructive one. They go together. They're much more extreme than the inner planets both in the best and the worst sense. Uranus embodies the human capacity to transform life through understanding and vision, through clarity of mind. It's where we part ways with the other kingdoms of nature, because no animal can look forward and envision a better future for itself. But Uranus also embodies the human capacity to destroy life because it isn't living up to the ideal of the better future. In mythology Uranus is merciless, he consigns his own children to the depths of Tartaros because he finds them too ugly and earthy.

Pluto I think embodies the power of nature to survive and to endure death and destruction without ever losing her creative potency. In nature nothing can ever be truly annihilated, because even if species become extinct, the life force continues and another better adapted species evolves. This kind of deathlessness is not spiritual immortality, but the sheer indestructibility of life. But Pluto also embodies the black heart of nature, which resists any attempt at cultivation and civilisation and wreaks revenge on any injury done her even if it's in the name of progress or development. Pluto embodies what the Furies meant in Greek myth, the revengeful powers of instinctual life which will not tolerate violation by an arrogant ego. If these are unleashed, then we compulsively destroy ourselves and each other, and that is nature's revenge.

Neptune embodies the deep inner wisdom that the human soul emanates from the divine, and that all living things are interconnected and part of one immense source of creative life. This is a profound experience of the heart, which of course cannot be proven in rational terms, but stands behind some of our highest ethics and our compassion for the rest of life. But I think Neptune also embodies the thing in us which refuses the responsibility for taking charge of our own lives, because Neptune would rather bask in the fountain of eternal grace and let someone else work and pay the bills and even suffer for us as long as we don't have to accept the loneliness of being human. The negative face of Neptune is a cannibal, who justifies any amount of manipulation and theft in the name of sacrifice and so-called love.

You can see that any strong contact with an outer planet can unleash both aspects of it. You can't have one without the other. There is always a treacherous element with the outer planets, which is why I become amused when astrologers think they're spiritual. When these planets get mixed up with Venus or hang about the seventh house or the eighth, then these extremes of experiences will come out in personal relationships. You can see why they cause so many problems to a more superficially minded person who hopes that everything will be alright if he can just be reasonable and talk things over with his partner. The outer planets are always as capable of destroying as they are of building. The only thing that can mediate them is the human ego with its values, because otherwise we are overwhelmed.

These are in many ways gods which are very unwelcome in the Judeo-Christian West. Uranus and Neptune and Pluto don't really fit religious dogma about the nature of God. If you follow an orthodox religion with any depth and seriousness, the outer planets can be an enormous problem, because they compel us into irrational behaviour and challenge conventional ethics. Of course it's immensely creative if you are involved with the arts, or if you deal with other people in depth, because strong outer planet contacts bring you to the root forces which drive the mass of humanity. But being aware of those things constitutes a kind of wound. The vision can never be actualised in any complete way, and there is always that potential for destruction. I sometimes feel that the inner planets are innocent in a curious way, even Mars, because they don't deal with what lies at the bottom of things. They aren't extreme.

Audience: Would you say the same about a semi-square?

Liz: A semi-square is like a diluted square. It's the same principle of friction, but not as compulsive. But yes, much of the same flavour is there, thinned out by two parts water.

Audience: And the quincunx?

Liz: Yes, any aspect to an outer planet brings one into contact with that energy. A quincunx is a very irritating aspect, because in some ways there is an attraction, the signs which are naturally in quincunx each have what the other lacks. But they suddenly repel each other, and I think it's a very erratic and irritating aspect. It isn't as pushy as the square family of aspects, and never degenerates into open conflict. I think it's a bit like one of those friendships where you really try to like each other and you some-times get on but somehow there are always little nasty remarks and a chilly atmosphere at the end of the evening. But if a quin-cunx involves an outer planet, then I think you must read it like any other aspect. An aspect is an enforced marriage between two principles which may or may not get on. And there can be no divorce.

Audience: I have Neptune on the descendant. Can you comment on that?

Liz: Any planet on the descendant concerns the image of the other, the expectations of the partner who will, one hopes, offer completeness. Planets at this cusp tend to be projected onto others. I think they belong to us, but they never really wholly feel like our own. We need another person to give them life and activate them. I think Neptune tends to produce a longing for the redeemer. One hopes that the other will be that magical, tender, elusive, divine creature who can raise one out of the muck and somehow convey an experience of oneness. I think another way of putting it is that one seeks the experience of the divine in the partner, which is always very dangerous. There are fantastic romantic ideals about relationship. One doesn't watch where one is going. The other person is never seen very clearly, but only through a rosy haze.

So of course there are experiences of disillusionment and dis-appointment, and often something must be sacrificed, because you aren't going to find God embodied in a human being to the extent that Neptune seeks it. This placement of Neptune has a funny reputation in textbooks, and is associated with deceit. I think the deceit only happens because of the wild idealism. If you really think you've married the Redeemer, then the poor partner can begin to stagger a bit under the load of the projection, because he or she can never be human. So often the partner goes off quietly, because it's nice to be approached on a flesh and blood level sometimes. Or disillusionment can drive the seventh house Neptune into looking elsewhere, hoping and hoping that the Redeemer will appear. I think by Redeemer I mean someone whose love can cleanse one of one's sins. That is a very common hope with Neptune. If only someone loved me enough, I wouldn't go on hating myself. It's a poor prognosis for relationships if one is unconscious of it. I think there can be a sensing of something divine or ecstatic in love, if one knows enough not to expect the partner to always be the embodiment of it.

Audience: Neptune is transiting across my midheaven at the moment. Would this affect my work, or partnerships since it's at the descendant in the birth chart?

Liz: I think it would affect both. The end result of the transit would be to bring about changes or realisations in your relationships with others. But the place of action, so to speak, would probably be your goals. The tenth house isn't just work. It's goals. It's the point where we seek to achieve something actively in the world. Neptune transiting in the midheaven suggests a great deal of confusion and disorientation, a change in goals and a feeling of muddle. I would guess that you used to know perfectly clearly where you wanted to go and now you're not so sure any more. Neptune brings longings out of us for what we can't have and can't even name. It might be that this change and loss of clear direction is bound up with a relationship, as if the other person were a catalyst of some kind. But perhaps it might give you a chance to give concrete form to something you have previously only looked for in other people.

Audience: My wife is a musician, and so am I, but I don't work professionally. But I've been feeling lately that we ought to work together at it.

Liz: I hope you do. I think this kind of thing is the glimpse of something that Neptune brings, and if you pursue it it will probably never be as glorious as you had imagined but it would be much more enriching than where you are now.

Audience: I have a Saturn-Uranus conjunction in the sixth house, which is very close to the seventh. Would you read that as in the sixth or the seventh? Do I have to have Uranian relationships?

Liz: Do you want me to tell you that yes, you must have them? It's not like prescribing a pill. It's probably you that secretly wants them. When a planet is very close to an angle like the descendant or the midheaven but is in the preceding house, it throws its influence into the next house and that is where its main effect lies. It's a bit like a person standing in a doorway looking into the next room. His presence is still around in the room he is leaving, but his main interest is in the room he's entering. And yes, I think Uranus will affect your relationship life. You surely don't need me to tell you that, most people are pretty aware of Uranus when it acts up. The complexity with you seems to lie in the combination of Uranus and Saturn. Saturn, as I said, is highly self-protective, and in terms of relationships it either avoids any deep and lasting commitment altogether by choosing safe or brief encounters, or it puts an over-emphasis on security and stability and rules within the relationship. Saturn always fears change, unless the person is controlling the change himself. I don't know whether you're liable to project Saturn on your partner, and blame him for restricting you, or whether you're likely to project Uranus, and blame him for being uncommitted. But you've got a nice dilemma between the need for secure, traditional structures and the need for exciting new encounters.

Uranus will usually overpower Saturn in the end, so that changes will occur either very literally or more subtly within your relationship life which force you to unbend a little and not be so suspicious of other people. Uranus in the seventh makes relationships the catalyst through which your ideas about yourself and about life change and evolve. I've seen people with Uranus in the seventh who always do the leaving, and I've also seen the reverse, where they are the ones who are left. But it's as though Uranus is saying, "Sorry, but nothing in life is as permanent as you try to make it." This of course hurts Saturn, who would like to freeze everything into granite so that one can't be hurt by life.

If you want to look at it in another way, I think that Uranus brings the sensitivity to the new vision into the sphere of relationship. What has worked for everybody else doesn't work for a seventh house Uranus, because it's always restlessly looking for new ways of dealing with others which are an improvement on the old institutions and attitudes. If you are unconscious of this, or feel threatened by it, then you will probably precipitate a breakup which forces you to face it anyway. If you know about it and try to work constructively with it, then it can help you build a very individual kind of relationship which is fulfilling but not dictated by other people's rules. With Saturn there you need something a little less wild than some seventh house Uranuses might like, but within a fairly conventional outer framework you need a very new kind of enactment with your partner.

I think that what we can solve within ourselves, or at least come to terms with, we can also offer to others. So my final comment on that placement is that probably you can develop a great deal of insight into the more general or universal problems of marriage and relationship because you would be so acutely aware of what is wrong between people. That can be a great gift if you work in any field that puts you in contact with others. I think it's interesting to remember that both Jung and Freud had Uranus in the seventh, and their insights into the dynamics of human interchange have opened up life for a great many people in a very new way.

Audience: What happens when the outer planets are unaspected?

Liz: I think I spoke about that in relation to Hitler's chart earlier. When a planet is unaspected, it becomes very difficult to know that it's there. It hides. Sooner or later it erupts. You don't have to deal with it constantly as people do who have it in strong aspect, but on those occasions when it does erupt it takes over your life for a time. I've noticed that when a planet is unaspected the person has a propensity for attracting partners who embody that planet, or whose birth placements trigger the unaspected planet. It's as though the sitting tenant in the basement would really like to be included in the life of the household but he's inarticulate and just doesn't know how to get upstairs, so he starts dropping bottles with messages in them out of the window. Other people pick up the bottles and knock on the front door. So you are indirectly pushed into discovering the thing which has been hiding.

Obviously the reasons why people become attracted to one another are enormously complex and very mysterious, and I don't think we will ever know all the answers. Plato called Eros a great *daimon,* and there is a very irrational thing at work in our attractions and repulsions which can never wholly be psychologised or analysed. But I think a great many relationships have parental roots, certainly in the earlier part of life. We tend to work out our mother and father problems and confusion about sexual identity on our partners, and it's pretty rare to see the partner as an actuality at all in the beginning of a relationship. All kinds of stuff gets projected from both sides, because we need these relationships to discover ourselves. I don't think there is such a thing as a normal relationship anyway, and when the outer planets get mixed up in it then you really have to throw away ideas about normal and abnormal.

The outer planets do suggest, however, that something more extensive than personal parental issues is being constellated. On the other hand our parents sometimes are experienced with the archetypal force of the outer planets, so they may still be mixed up in it. But relationships which are outer-planet prone have a very strange, compulsive, exhilarating feeling about them, both for good and for ill. There is a feeling of fate. Outer planets don't always mean multiple marriages, they are perfectly capable of sticking with the same partner. But the relationship itself is generally unusual in some way, or goes through many changes and transformations which shake the whole life. There are people for whom partners are like furniture, meant to be sat on or dined on at the proper hour and then left to gather dust in the interim. You cannot do this when outer planets are connected with Venus or the seventh house.

The feeling of destiny is sometimes very strong, and I have heard many people use similar expressions when talking about a relationship which feels "meant." It can't be avoided. Uranus in particular has a disturbing habit of seeing somebody on the other side of the room and knowing with great finality that this is it. Usually we get over the idea of instantaneous love after a few bruises and the discovery that it takes a long time to get to know somebody else. But Uranus knows immediately and whatever problems ensue, that same feeling of destiny hangs around, even if the relationship doesn't work out. I'm not sure what "meant" means, except that the other person is the necessary trigger for psychic growth. The frightening side of this is the feeling that one is not in control. That is quite true, we aren't in control when the outer planets are around. The ego does not like the feeling of being borne along on a current without a paddle. So however wonderful and ecstatic the experience is, there is a great uneasiness and a fear that it might suddenly turn nasty. The fear is much greater if you're a more Saturnian or earthy temperament, for obvious reasons.

It's worth remembering that the three outer planets have elemental affinities and are therefore more or less acceptable to individuals depending on their general birth chart pattern. Uranus is an airy planet, and I think it's much more welcome to an airy temperament. I think water signs have quite a horror of Uranus because it so often brings separations. Just the inner experience of separation is horrible to many watery people, even if the partner is sitting in the next chair preoccupied with his own thoughts. Water needs to feel in touch all the time, and Uranus tends to just go off into the ethers. Neptune and Pluto, on the other hand, rule watery signs, and although they are still likely to be difficult, they aren't as alien to watery types as they are to the air signs. Gemini and Libra and Aquarius are very light and idealistic and clear, and Pluto's brand of seething murk is definitely not attractive to them. Neptune is disturbing and frightening because of the fogginess and loss of clarity and feeling of enchantment. The air signs are not in favour of living in a magical world of spells and intuitions and strange visions. They like to know the reasons for things.

I think the element of fire is very inimical to Saturn, but it's less disturbed by Pluto and Neptune. Uranus is fine for fire as long as the changes which ensue are not cramping or limiting. But fire of all the elements is least frightened by the unexpected, because fire tends to busily rush about wondering what it all means and looking for future potentialities in the new situation. Earth is probably least comfortable with the outer planets in general because they represent the unknown and earth is safe with known facts. I have found that very earthy astrologers get very alarmed by outer planet transits, because they start making concrete predictions. Everything is experienced in concrete terms. And not every event is concrete. There are very potent emotional and mental events which don't touch the body or the external circumstances, but which alter the soul.

Fire, which I think symbolises what Jung means by intuition, has a great many failings in ordinary life, but it has one great advantage in terms of the outer planets, and that is the love of the new. I have seen many fire sign clients talk about their hunch that some big change is coming, when a transit of an outer planet is shown in the chart. The client may know no astrology, but he senses something and starts preparing for it. That is a great help with the outer planets because an attitude of open expectation is probably the best. But of course no chart is purely fiery, and there is always some area of fear. Nevertheless I think we can all learn from the typical fiery approach, even though there is no such thing as a purely fiery person. This approach is really hamfisted when trying to get on with the issues of everyday living, but it's great with the outer planets.

Audience: In other words, if you have an outer planet transit coming, suspend your air sign judgments and your water sign likes and dislikes, and wait hopefully to see what happens.

Liz: Exactly. Since all three outer planets are very slow and do their retrograde dance a few times over any point in the chart, there's lots of time to get accustomed to what the transit might mean. Some older writers such as Alan Leo tend to refer to Neptune and Uranus as malefic. Alan Leo didn't know about Pluto, but I'm sure he would have thought Pluto was the most malefic of all. Sometimes there are very difficult experiences that come with these planets, and sometimes tragedy. But "malefic" implies that they have bad intent and bad effect, and although it's easy for me to say and hard for anyone to live, even the tragedies that occur under the outer planets are meaningful and can open up life if we allow it. It seems to me a fairly jaundiced view on the part of astrology to figure that anything beyond the seven known planets has got to be nasty. I have never been convinced that transits put into a life what isn't innately potentially there anyway.

So yes, I think it's very important to suspend judgment if one is trying to understand the effects of these planets. This is particularly true when they erupt into relationships. If you are in the middle of a very compulsive experience and there is an outer planet involved, it isn't of very much help to wonder whether you should or you shouldn't. You probably won't find an answer. It might be more relevant to ask what it means to you, before you make any far-reaching decisions or judgments. One of the functions of the outer planets is that they crack the shell of conventional morality, in order to allow a different and deeper kind of morality to emerge. Or another way of putting it is that they push a person into discovering what his real morality is, rather than what he thought it was.

One of the most interesting cross-aspects that I have found in chart comparison is Saturn in one person's chart contacting one of the outer planets in another's. Someone asked earlier about a Saturn-Pluto contact across two charts. The scenario is fascinating, and can also be quite devastating if you are the one caught in it instead of astrologising about it. Outer planets really bring the conservative element out of Saturn. The Saturnian person may have previously been quite liberal and free, but the moment he gets around an outer planet in his partner's chart he suddenly becomes very tight. He begins to make comments about the partner's eccentricities. Even if he does precisely the same things himself, he will find something to criticise. Sometimes this comes out in the smallest ways, such as criticism about eating habits or dress or one's weird friends. I have seen this in really unconventional people who are the last ones to be accused of Saturnian rigidity. But when Saturn is threatened by the outer planets then this very conservative quality comes to the surface. We all have Saturn in the chart, and we all therefore have a level of respect and need for social mores. Whether this is conscious or unconscious, nevertheless it's there in us all. It's as well that it is, or we would have no sense of social responsibility or order. But outer planets tend to bring it out in an extreme form. Saturn becomes threatened, and his first offering is his disapproval.

The Saturnian person may then try to stifle the partner. He may actively try to prevent some part of the other person's expression, or make his disapproval so clear that the partner feels intimidated. I think that Saturn tends to feel rather irrelevant in the face of Uranus, Neptune and Pluto. Of course if you perpetually try to obstruct something that volatile in another, then eventually the other person becomes increasingly resentful and rebellious. You can see the same curious transformation at work. An ordinary sedate, conventional, ordinary person begins to become increasingly Uranian, or Neptunian, or Plutonian, in the face of Saturnian pressure. Uranus may show overt rebellion, or simply walk out. Neptune begins to become increasingly evasive, and starts fighting back with atmospheres and emotional manipulation and a covert implication that you are really being terribly petty and mean and thick. Pluto may strike back through sexual games, or through hatred. If one falls into the outer planet, one can lose all sense of the value of the relationship, because the destructive side of the outer planet has been unleashed. Then it moves beyond your control, and you act out the outer planet for the other person.

You can see that it takes a lot of effort to see what's going on in this kind of interchange. I am inclined to go back again to the need for emotional honesty, especially with oneself. I think a lot of responsibility falls on the shoulders of the Saturn person, because it is his personal fears and insecurities which set the ball rolling.

Audience: It would be interesting to see the charts of the people with whom Hitler was closely involved, to see whether his unaspected Neptune and Pluto were strongly affected.

Liz: Yes, I would be interested in that too, although I don't have horoscopes for Eva Braun and Himmler and the rest of the pack.

Audience: What orbs do you allow in synastry?

Liz: I tend to use fairly large ones, no different from the orbs within a natal chart. I know that isn't usually acceptable, but it seems to me to work. In practise, I think eight degree orbs for a conjunction across charts definitely produce a reaction. There is perhaps less compulsiveness about wider orbs, just as with a natal chart, but that doesn't mean the connection isn't there. Close orbs in synastry are immediately recognisable. If you meet someone at a party for the first time, and you have some exact aspects between the two charts, then you will react strongly right from the outset. But the more you get to know someone, the more the wider orbs come into play. If you live with a person, or are a member of the family, then the bigger orbs are definitely operative. If you only see someone at seminars once every two weeks and never talk to them about much except the weather, then those wider orbs are not noticeable. I think you must look at what kind of relationship it is. Some aspects aren't really relevant if the relationship is of a very circumscribed kind. They just don't have a chance to come into play. But I think in general that we constrict our orbs too much in synastry work. This is particularly true about the sun and moon.

Audience: What about Saturn?

Liz: Yes, Saturn as well. Saturn is a very powerful planet, and I think it's as important as the sun and moon. I've always felt that the sun and Saturn tell you about the spinal column of the birth chart. Both planets pertain to the ego, in its creative and its defensive aspects. The sun and Saturn are the bedrock of the personality.

Audience: What aspects would you particularly look at in comparing two charts?

Liz: Any aspects. I think minor aspects such as the semisquare and semisextile and sesquiquadrate operate within relationships just as much as the major ones do. In progressions, you learn very quickly that minor aspects are very important. It's a mistake to overlook them. Progressed minor aspects trigger off major natal aspects.

Audience: Do you use composite charts? And if so, how would you read the outer planets in a composite chart?

Liz: I do work with composite charts, despite the fact that they irritate me in principle because they ought not to work. But they are uncannily truthful about describing the main areas of focus and conflict in a relationship, and they are even sensitive to transits. Even worse, you can do a synastry between a composite chart and a third party, and it reveals a lot about how the third party will affect the relationship. I find composite charts quite extraordinary. But they offend me because there is something so impersonal about them. They describe an entity which doesn't really have any volition to change. It just exists in an abstract form. You can set up a composite chart between yourself and Cosimo de' Medici, and it would be perfectly valid even though he's been dead for six hundred years. This bothers me. A composite chart describes something which has an existence independent of the human souls which blend to create it. It's almost like a machine.

I think the outer planets have the same meaning in a composite chart as they do in an individual one. But there is no real link with an ego which can work with them. I think Uranus implies the sphere of the relationship where two people will experience separateness, freedom from the relationship, and disruptions from uncontrollable sources. Neptune, I would say, suggests the sphere where sacrifices must be made, where too much idealism leads to expectations that cannot be wholly fulfilled and lead to disappointment. And Pluto I think deals with the sphere of life which because of its problems and conflicts leads to change or transformation in both people involved in the relationship.

So far as I have seen, these placements in composite charts do work out within the relationship. The thing that bothers me, as I have said, is the feeling of inevitability about it. All one can do is be aware that something in the chemistry of the relationship is going to lead to benefits and conflicts in particular areas. Maybe then both people can try to allow the relationship to stretch enough to hold these things, rather than being surprised by them when they come to the surface. But perhaps it's necessary to accept that certain aspects of our relationships are fated or inevitable, and that life is a blend of choices and necessities. Jung once described free will as the ability to do gladly what one must do, and I suppose the composite chart shows what one must do in terms of a relationship while the other type of synastry—comparing cross-aspects and so on—describes the areas where we can bring consciousness to bear and change things. We are fated by what we are, and if two people come together, their individual natures in combination are going to produce certain inevitable results.

Lecture Seven

I would like to begin this session with a rather curious map, which is the idea or design of Gret Baumann-Jung, Jung's daughter. She is an astrologer, and she devised this particular map, so I claim no credit for it whatsoever. But I find it very interesting, although it is in many ways a kind of intuitive way of looking at things rather than something very pragmatic which can be statistically proven. It's a way of mapping an astrological age, to get a sense of where the emphasis will lie in terms of values, ethics, conflicts, and change in different spheres of life during the 2100 or so years that form the astrological aeon.

What she does is place the sign which rules the age on the ascendant of the horoscope, and then all the other signs follow in order around the wheel. We can start by doing this with the Piscean Age which according to our traditions is just in process of its last gasps.

You can see that if Pisces is placed here on the cusp of the first house, then Aries falls on the second. This suggests that the general collective attitudes toward second house matters during the Piscean Age—money, security, stability—are going to carry a certain aggressive, one-pointed, self-centered quality. Taurus falls on the cusp of the third house, so the mental attitudes are pragmatic and based on perception by the senses. Knowledge or wisdom acquired through other modes of perception is not really acceptable to Taurus, because its strong point is dealing with material reality. This gives you some idea of the general way of working with such a map. Scorpio appears on the cusp of the ninth house, so the general collective attitudes toward religious matters will be emotionally rather than rationally based, very intense, perhaps dogmatic and even warlike. I think you can see that history bears these generalisations out, because in the case of the last sign mentioned, no other astrological age has produced religions which are so passionately intolerant and ready to slaughter anything resembling heresy than the great religions of the Piscean Age. And Leo, the sign which is most related to the principle of individuality, falls on the cusp of the sixth house, which suggests that the route toward individual consciousness and development has focused on work, on duty, and on the rituals of ordinary life.

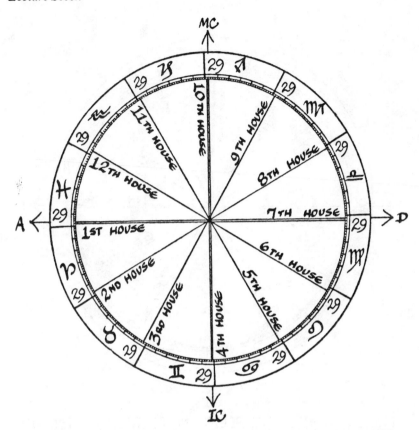

Illustration 13: THE BEGINNING OF THE PISCEAN AGE

Having given you this rough idea of how to work with the map, we can try putting Aquarius on the ascendant to get a sense of how things are likely to change.

Here Leo, which was previously found on the sixth house cusp, now turns up on the seventh. That implies that just as in the Piscean Age the individual value was found in mundane life and its rituals and obligations, now in the Aquarian Age the individual value and development is to be found in human relationships and the balancing of opposites. As a kind of intuitive suggestion of where we might expect change, I find this rather hopeful, because rather than finding meaning only in your job and

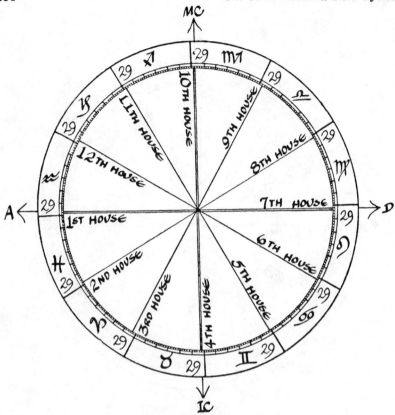

Illustration 14: THE BEGINNING OF THE AQUARIAN AGE

your small daily concerns, it can now be found in interchange with the other, both externally and internally. I think depth psychology is certainly pointing in this direction—that relationship both outer and inner, rather than good works and meticulous observation of duty, is the path of individual development.

It also might be interesting to look at what happens to Capricorn, which in the Piscean Age chart falls on the eleventh house cusp, and here in the Aquarian Age chart comes up on the cusp of the twelfth. I would take this to mean that the sense of limitation and bondage and obstruction—the experience of the shadow —has fallen on the shoulders of "other people" in the Piscean Age, so that the collective feeling is about the obstruction of other countries, other political parties, other social groups. Now it lands squarely in a house which deals with the unconscious, particularly the collective unconscious, as if the realisation might finally dawn that the enemy lies within and is an accruing of many aeons of collective conflict and murk inside. The limitations of life are experienced from within, rather than in the form of other people, as if we might at last take up the burden of our own ambivalent and complex human natures.

Now, that's a sort of introduction to the chart. What one does next is plot the transiting planets across it. The transits of the inner planets are of course going to shoot by incredibly quickly, and they won't make much noise in the course of two thousand years. But the transits of the outer planets are much slower, and one can expect, during the course of a lifetime, to see them emphasising some area of conflict in the collective. Uranus takes about seven years to move through a sign, so it will make the round of this chart in eighty-four years, and spend those seven years in one house. Neptune will spend around fourteen years in one house, and Pluto a varying time from eighteen to thirty years. That's long enough to see some manifestation of this activity. This gives a sense of an underlying rhythm, a rise and fall of new ideas, movements and visions arising from the collective, which cycle around the "world horoscope" many times during the course of the age.

So we might look first at Pluto, which is in Libra at the moment and would be found somewhere in the eighth house of the chart, if we assume that the ascendant is now the very earliest degrees of Pisces or the very last degrees of Aquarius. Don't forget that we are moving backward with the ages, not forward.

Uranus has been moving through the ninth while in Scorpio, if we take 0 degrees of Scorpio as the cusp of that house, and Neptune is somewhere in the tenth. Pluto going through the eighth house suggests to me that profound changes have been occurring for some time in our attitudes toward sexuality and in our confrontations with the primitive or instinctual depths of ourselves. Once Pluto moves into Scorpio it will begin to affect matters of religion, but there are still a couple of years to go while it completes its radical transformation of our hidden animal natures. Put in simpler terms, the last twenty years or so have seen a revolution in our attitudes toward sex, whereas once Pluto enters Scorpio the next twenty will see a revolution in our forms of worshipping God. Uranus has already been exploding things in the religious sphere, and I cannot help but make a connection with the eruption of "fundamentalist" movements such as that happening in Islam. In the last few years new sects of a revolutionary kind have been proliferating all over America. There is a real boom in eccentric offshoot religions at the moment. That will probably quiet down when Uranus moves into Sagittarius, and then Pluto not long after will begin its slow and more profound undermining of our collective religious structures and standards. When Uranus moves into the tenth it will no doubt lead to changes in styles of government and reshifting of class structures and political party systems, because those are tenth house matters.

Now perhaps it might be interesting to plot our conjunction in Capricorn on this chart, that we have been discussing over the course of the weekend. Previously we looked at this conjunction in terms of the charts of particular countries, and in terms of psychological meaning of such a line-up for the deeper collective. Here in this chart for the end of the Piscean Age and the beginning of the Aquarian, the line-up falls in the eleventh. I think the most general meaning of the eleventh is that it represents the human family, the group. It's also the goals and ideals of the group, in terms of the evolution of consciousness and the development of society into a better vehicle for human beings to live their lives. So all the things we have envisioned for ourselves as the proper and ethical development of social groups, our visions of the ideal society, must change profoundly. It's as though we will have to conceive of the nature of man differently, because all our efforts for a "better world" have been based on certain assumptions made about man as a social animal with certain needs and characteristics, and many of these may be found to be wrong or outdated.

When Uranus and Neptune and Saturn conjuncted in Scorpio in 1307, they fell in the ninth house of this chart for the Piscean Age. I think I expressed my feeling of what happened on a collective level at that time—the unshakeable belief in the Church and the infallibility of the Pope were dealt a death-blow. Appropriately, this is a ninth house matter. It would be hard to imagine that it could be anything except a ninth house matter. That is a very clear and rather disturbing example of the fact that this chart, although it seems such a wild and speculative piece of intuitive vision, actually works. In a few years Pluto will enter

Scorpio while the other three heavy planets are playing about in Capricorn, and Pluto will then take its turn through the ninth house—which, at the dawn of the Aquarian Age, would have twenty-nine degrees of Libra on its cusp. This suggests something even more momentous in terms of religious changes, because Pluto doesn't just alter aspects of something. It wipes out the entire thing and begins again. Pluto has of course been through the ninth house before, since it makes its round in two hundred and forty-eight years. But it hasn't passed through the ninth house at the start of the Aquarian Age, when new religious images and directions are likely to be emerging from the collective anyway.

The sign of the age, the sign which falls on the ascendant of this "world horoscope," represents I think something very similar to what it represents in an individual horoscope. The ascendant is the thing toward which we strive, the glimpse of the divine toward which life drives us. Often this is acknowledged very reluctantly, and I have met many people who dislike their rising signs, largely because this sign represents something they must come to terms with whether they approve or not. But it's as though God, or life, formulates itself into experiences which are typical of the sign on the ascendant, and those are the things which make one grow and for which, if one is honest, one longs. An astrological age is no different, really. The stamp of the Piscean Age was, in many ways, the longing for union with the divine, and the escape from the mortality and corruption and darkness of earthly life. Life through the eyes of Pisces is at best something to be shaped into a worship of God, not something which is good and beautiful in itself. The three great religions which were founded under the Piscean Age—Christianity, Buddhism and Islam—all carry this theme in one way or another. The stamp of the Aquarian Age is of course likely to be very different, and our religious needs are likely to change accordingly. Spirit and matter are not so split for Aquarius as they are for Pisces. God is alive in matter and reveals itself as the laws of nature and the laws in particular of human nature. I think it's possible that Pluto's transit through Scorpio in the 'eighties and 'nineties will give us some idea of the shape of religion in the future.

The great conjunction of 1524, which scared all the astrologers half to death, would have fallen in the first house of the chart, right across the ascendant. This was a conjunction of sun, moon, Mercury, Venus, Mars, Jupiter, Saturn and Neptune, although they

of course didn't know about Neptune. This conjunction coincided
with the dawn of the Reformation. That implies that the currents
at work behind the issues of the Reformation were not so much a
ninth house matter as a first house matter, a defining or redefining
of the Christian myth in more conscious terms. That is what I
think happens when important transits occur across the ascendant.
We are forced to redefine our experience of ourselves and what we
are really like. The dominant issue of the Reformation to my
mind was the problem of whether man needs the edifice of the
Church as his sole route to God, or whether he is capable of rely-
ing on his own inner guidance and conscience. There wasn't really
any question about the validity of the Christian myth—but rather
a question of whether individuals had the right to interpret it
individually. That is much more a first house matter than a ninth.

Very often the first place one sees new issues emerging from
the collective is in the dreams of individuals. Jung wrote extensively about this in relation to the dreams of his German patients
before the outbreak of the last war. He knew from these dreams
that something monumental and very dangerous was about to
burst loose from the collective psyche, which he felt was connected with the ancient Teutonic deity Wotan who had been long
neglected and seemed to be stirring again. I suspect that if there
are new religious forms or symbols of collective import then they
are going to cast their shadows before them in the dreams of
individuals now. I can't really comment on this, because I don't
think I have been observing it for long enough, but one of the
most consistent themes which I keep running across is a very
angry feminine deity who seems to wish to become conscious
and acknowledged. I will leave you to think about that one,
because it is only my intuition. But I have a very strong feeling
that whatever religious crises or dilemmas arise at the dawn of
the new era, one of the main components is going to be problems of the feminine aspect of the godhead, which hasn't been
given a lot of notice for the last two thousand years.

I know that there are a lot of images around in dreams as well
as in clairvoyants' visions of earthquakes and tidal waves and
other gigantic catastrophes. I cannot comment on whether these
things are literal or not, because I'm not clairvoyant, and even if
I were I wouldn't jump at the idea that they were necessarily
concrete. I have met these motifs in individuals' dreams, and they
indicate a tremendous upheaval in the unconscious. These kinds of

dreams almost always herald major transformations in the person-ality, and the ego often feels terrified and threatened because new elements are going to come to the surface and old attitudes are going to die. The enormity of the catastrophe reflects the enor-mity of the threat to the ego's old standpoint. Sometimes dreams like this imply a danger that the ego may be swamped, but I don't think they state that it will be—only that it could be, if it isn't understanding what is required. I am inclined, therefore, to take these pronouncements of clairvoyants as though they were dreams, since I think both come from the unconscious, and I feel they reflect an enormous upheaval in the collective uncon-scious which could, but doesn't have to, swamp the ego, or in collective terms, the structures of society. The person who is in touch with this realm and can sense the upheaval is, in astrological terms, someone who can tap the twelfth house.

Audience: Can you comment on the association of the twelfth with the house of karma?

Liz: Karma is a very difficult word, because I think we have dis-torted it enormously from its original meaning. Karma in Indian thought is the principle of cause and effect. It has no particular morality attached to it, since all occurrences in the world belong to the realm of illusion anyway, "good" deeds as well as "bad." Man sows his seed without thought or consciousness of the con-sequences, and then later he must reap what he has sown. It is a law of nature, not a system of reward and punishment. When Theosophy got its hands on the idea of karma, it was sifted through the peculiar morality of late Victorian thought, and it became a kind of ding-dong idea. If you did something bad in your last life, then you got punished in this one, and if you were good and moral, then you reaped rewards in this one. I think this is a horrible distortion of a much more profound idea which links up with what the Greeks called *heimarmene*, the chain of eternal causation in nature. We cannot see that chain of causes because its roots lie in matter itself. Karma in this sense is about substance. Like attracts like. You are made of particular substance through a chain of endless causes which may be your past lives or may be your heredity or may be the eternal interaction of life on the planet. This is the substance of which you are made, and you will attract in life those people and situations which are made of similar substance. It's a bit like playing a note on a guitar and having it picked up by a nearby tuning fork, which is attuned to the same pitch. As Jung puts it, a man's life is characteristic of himself.

If you look at karma in this way, then the entire horoscope is karmic, because it describes your substance. I think that the twelfth house carries the connotation of that part of your substance which stems from the past. As to which past, I would be hard-pressed to say, because the past of a family is just as potent as the possible past of other incarnations. Family ghosts and myths and unresolved complexes are incredibly potent powers, and so are racial and national pressures which have been accruing over centuries. Perhaps there really isn't any conflict between the idea of psychological family inheritance and past life inheritance, since presumably one gets the family one deserves. But I think the twelfth house describes this realm of *heimarmene*, the unseen chain of causation that stretches back into the past, the past of the family, of the nation, of the race. If there are planets in the twelfth house in the birth chart, then they will not only describe the individual's needs. They will also describe him as expressing the needs of the collective from which he springs. He embodies his family past, and he must create his life within the limitations of this inherited package.

If a person is sensitive to this deep underlying stratum of life, then he will in a sense be carrying group karma. But I want to stress that I don't mean the term in any moral sense. He is carrying group substance, family substance. He can't just go off and try to lead a completely independent and self-made life. There are larger, more collective issues which he must come to terms with, before he is allowed to go free. I think this is the connotation of bondage which is so often associated with the twelfth. It's bond-to collective issues from the past which must be faced and worked with creatively. This isn't any more "karmic" than having lots of planets in the second house and therefore having to come to terms with material reality and money and self-sufficiency. It just feels stranger when it's the twelfth because it isn't your own. It's collective.

I have found that people with strongly tenanted twelfth houses often feel terribly lonely, because they live with undercurrents and perceptions that most of us never see and don't know exist. I have known some of these people to have a rare gift of sensing the soul of a place, the long past which lives in a house or a part of the landscape. I made the acquaintance of someone with several planets in the twelfth who couldn't bear to drive through northern France, because this part of France is so soaked in the blood of so many wars over so many centuries. For her it was a reality, and an unbearable experience, whereas anyone else would have called her hysterical. I think that the events of history and the experiences of human souls leave residues, and these residues linger and themselves become causes for the behaviour of the people who afterward live in those places. The twelfth house senses all these things. The problem is that the person often doesn't know what it is that's affecting him so strongly. He just feels crazy, and other people's rationality makes him doubt his own perceptions.

I'm not really sure what this might have to do with the kinds of changes which we can expect over the next few decades. But I would like to believe, I suppose, that the worlds of the eleventh and twelfth houses, which really in the end deal with the interconnectedness of life and the unseen world of archetypal dominants, are going to make their entry into our vocabulary. That would indeed be the end of a world and the beginning of a new one. I don't feel this is an issue of "spirituality" so much as an issue of consciousness. Much of that unseen world is very dark, and certainly isn't just benign and light and full of love and compassion. But it belongs to life nevertheless. I would also like to believe that I can see the incipient signs of this in individuals. I've been doing charts for seventeen years, and once upon a time, when I started, people came because they were in trouble caused by life, other people, outside situations. It was extremely rare to meet anyone wanting a horoscope who right from the outset was prepared to view his own psyche as the initiator of his trouble. Also, it was extremely rare to meet anyone who didn't have a sense of shame or failure because of his conflicts. We have been brought up to believe that the natural state of man is harmony and placidity, and that if an inner opposition or conflict arose, it meant one was sick.

I have found that this has changed over the last few years. I have met more and more people seeking help who are prepared to look at their own role in their trouble. I have also met more and more people who are aware that conflict is inherent in the human psyche, and that there is no shame or admission of guilt in acknowledging it and wishing to learn more about it. I find this terribly encouraging. I would like to believe that it reflects a very subtle but very important change beginning in the collective, which is very much about taking responsibility for the fact that our lives are characteristic of ourselves. Naturally if you take this to its obvious conclusion it doesn't herald an age of love and brotherhood, but more likely an age of a great deal of individual agony. But I can't help feeling that if I am prepared to work with my own agony, and you are prepared to work with yours, then maybe the collective won't have to plunge itself into blind agony. At the moment all our family scapegoats, the schizophrenics and the anorexics and the depressives, act out all our collective pain, while the rest of us get on with it blandly and free of conflict. Think what it would mean if each of us confronted our own individual psychosis. You see why it's easier to drop the subject, and even to use astrology as a means of escape.

Audience: When does the Piscean Age actually end and the Aquarian Age actually begin?

Liz: There is considerable argument about that. I doubt that one can be very exact. The decision about which star marks the end of the constellation of Pisces and the beginning of the constellation of Aquarius is not one I would care to make. I think it's possible to talk in terms of an overlap, which lasts for perhaps a century. I have heard many dates given. For all I know the Aquarian Age began last Tuesday. I feel it's more creative to think of this century as a transitional one. There is a smell of decay rising from the fading body of Pisces, and a smell of rising sap from the ongoing birth of Aquarius, and I think at the moment they're very mixed up together.

Audience: I can't help feeling slightly upset at what you are saying. We keep reading that the new age is about the brotherhood of man.

Liz: No doubt it is, but if that's the vision which is emerging from the collective, then we must first go through the long and bloody process of discovering why we have never been able to experience brotherhood. No individual becomes conscious of himself instantaneously and without suffering, and no collective does either.

The psyche just doesn't work like that. If something must die, then it's going to raise a hell of a fuss in the process, and if something is being born, it's going to cause pain to the thing giving it birth. You can give a woman an anaesthetic when she is giving birth to a baby, but you can't anaesthetise the soul, not without paying an awful price. I'm afraid I'm a little jaundiced about all these hopes for the age of love and brotherhood arriving next month. It's a bit like getting married in a beautiful dress with a wonderful bouquet of flowers and then believing that because you have just married, you will now understand marriage and be able to live the symbol immediately. No marriage works like that, and I don't think the Aquarian Age does either. It may be that Aquarius will bring us the awareness that we are indeed part of a vast interconnected life entity, both biologically and psychologically. But the awareness is going to force up everything in us which obstructs us from living our vision. Jung thought the Aquarian Age was about the final collision between good and evil, and if I understand him properly I think he means, as usual, the collision of these opposites within the individual. That is more in line with what I would imagine than what we have been told by our more mystically inclined astrology books. We have an enormous challenge on our hands, and an enormous struggle, the outcome of which I am sure is not yet determined. We're beginning to introject God, and that's horribly dangerous as well as being potentially creative.

I associate Aquarius with the myth of Prometheus. He is the Titan who steals fire from Zeus to give to mankind. Prometheus is committing a sin, because he brings man divine consciousness, which Zeus has deliberately withheld because he doesn't want man to realise that he has the same divine spark as the gods. Now Prometheus has done a very noble deed, he's the great mythic social worker, and he is punished horribly for it and bears his punishment unflinchingly. But he's also a fool, because he doesn't take into account what man might do with his fire. Man might inflate and blow the gods right out of heaven, and blow himself up as well. There is always great danger in the increase of consciousness, because the shadow can appropriate the new gifts for its own purposes, and only the terribly frail voice of inner conscience and inner integrity can put up a fight. I wouldn't trust Prometheus, and I don't trust the outcome of the Aquarian Age as a necessarily foregone and wonderful paradise on earth.

There are many references made to the text of *Revelation* in terms of the dawning of the new age. If one reads *Revelation* psychologically, I think it describes the rising up of the collective shadow, which we have seen already in this century and will no doubt see a good deal more of unless it can be handled individually. If this great upsurge of darkness is not to happen in the collective, then it must happen in the individual, in each of us one by one. That is what I understand by Jung's idea of the confrontation of good and evil. There are other prophetic texts around which also seem to describe a similar collective event. Nostradamus is of course one of the more famous prophets, and Malachi is another interesting one.

Malachi was concerned exclusively with the destiny of the Church, which of course in his day, the twelfth century, was the only one. He seems to have had a vision of the precise number of Popes, and after he has listed them and attributed a particular image or symbol to each one, he prophesies that there will no longer be a Pope in Rome. What he means is not very clear. He might be prophesying the end of the Catholic Church, or he might be describing its transformation. Once again I find it helpful to take him symbolically, even though he is so apparently concrete and specific in his prophecies. The Pope is not just a physical person, he is also Christ's Vicar, the intermediary between man and God. In Malachi's day, there was no other route to God. If there is no longer an intermediary, how are man and God to meet each other? If a person dreams that the Pope dies or is no more, then I would be inclined to read into it a movement toward a more direct experience of the spirit, and the end of an externalised projection of spiritual authority. That is not to say that there should or should not be an actual Pope. But taken internally, I think it's a statement about direct experience of the spirit.

Nostradamus seems to have concerned himself with a much broader spectrum than just the Papacy. His prophecies have continued to baffle people since the sixteenth century, and many of them are ambiguous enough to interpret in just about any way you like. But he does seem to have been rather gloomy about the last decades of the twentieth century. Although he combined his apparent clairvoyance with astrology, he would not have known about the conjunction of Uranus, Neptune and Saturn, because Uranus and Neptune hadn't been discovered. The conjunctions which preoccupied him were Jupiter and Saturn, and also Mars

and Saturn. Nevertheless he thought some monumental catastrophe was due at the end of this century, followed by some
kind of golden age. Once again there is a proliferation of images
of a great upheaval in the collective. The collapse of the Papacy
also seems to have occupied Nostradamus, but once again I am
inclined to take it more symbolically.

Poets are also prophets, and one of the more powerful prophecies I have read is W. B. Yeats' poem, *The Second Coming*.
Yeats was also very versed in astrology, and he was very particularly writing about the changing of the astrological ages. The
poem begins, naturally, with a description of disintegration
and upheaval in the collective, and the advent of a "rough beast"
with the head of a man and the body of a lion—Leo and Aquarius
being the opposites for the new age. This poem is not a prophecy about an age of love and brotherhood, but about collective
turmoil and chaos and the emergence of a new religious vision
"slouching toward Bethlehem to be born."

I am sorry if I have upset anyone with these things, but it is
perhaps wiser to be realistic. I think if one just does horoscopes
and reads Theosophical books, then it all seems so easy. But we
are not easy, we are terribly complex, all of us, and anyone with
any experience of psychotherapy will know that you cannot force
growth. The psyche has its own laws and there is a great dis-
crepancy between what we are and what we would like to be. I
am in no way pessimistic, only realistic. It would be nice if we had
Aquarian Age pills which would magically transform us all into
the sort of people Aquarians like to envisage. But the problem
of love isn't really solvable by idealistic thinking. That is surely
apparent to you all.

I had a rather strange experience a few years ago apropos this
issue of Pisces and Aquarius and the particular viewpoints of the
different astrological ages. I had occasion to attend a conference
at that time, which was meant to be a sort of gathering of pro-
fessional people in various psychological, spiritual and alternative
healing fields. The subject of the conference was the Aquarian
Age. There were two extraordinary speakers at this conference.
I will not mention names, although some of you will no doubt
recognise the first one, as he tends to attract a fair amount of
publicity to himself. He spoke about the Second Coming of Christ,
He addressed us in a reassuring, intimate, soothing voice, and told
us how Christ was going to return with his disciples. He presented

this happening as a concrete event, a recurrence of what happened two thousand years ago, as though it were an exact repetition which would take place despite the modern world with its technology, its cynicism, its agnosticism and its jadedness with gurus and spiritual truths. He was certainly a very powerful and charismatic speaker, although being rather pagan in sympathy I have yet to be convinced of the First Coming, let alone the Second. Nevertheless I will listen to anything once.

The second speaker then proceeded to tell us about the existence of extraterrestrial beings who were at this very moment preparing to land on earth. He was not in the least bit religious in the ordinary sense, but spoke with considerable technological acumen about the nature of the spaceships and the methods by which they had already made telepathic contact with particular human beings. He saw this great imminent event in the same terms as the first speaker saw his vision of the Second Coming. Both expected it to herald the dawn of the Aquarian Age, and both thought it meant the subsequent spiritual enlightenment of mankind.

I found this juxtaposition quite fascinating. Both of these men were attempting to describe the same thing, but in totally opposite metaphors. One saw the imminent change in straight Biblical terms, complete with miracles and attendant phenomena. The other saw it in straight technological terms, scientifically explicable and rational. These different metaphors were no doubt right and appropriate for the different psyches of the two men. I felt that one spoke in the metaphor of the Piscean Age, and the other in the metaphor of the Aquarian. But both were attempting to articulate a kind of inner vision. Perhaps they were both awfully concrete about this vision. I would be inclined to see it that way, because an event only assumes such cosmic proportions if a myth is being born synchronous with the event. For that reason I am much more interested in the birth of the Christian myth at the beginning of the Piscean era, than I am in the birth of an historical personage called Jesus. If that sounds anti-Christian, I assure you it isn't, it's just anti-literalness.

But this thing which the one gentleman called the Second Coming is a vision which is increasingly prevalent. A very large number of people attend this man's lectures, and contribute large sums of money toward his enterprise. I would not in any way mock the anticipation of such an event. But I would suggest that it is an inner event rather than an outer one, and I would go even further and suggest that it is already happening within individuals. That little spark of increased responsibility and recognition of an inner and very mysterious process is to me the signpost of the Second Coming, although not in any sense that a more Biblical-minded person might understand it. It's such a small and humble thing, that little bit of consciousness. One sees it in analytic work, the long slow sifting through such apparently banal and mundane and intimate life details, and the growing feeling that somewhere inside is an orderly pattern, a Something which is the creative shaper of one's life. I do hope there will be UFO landings, I think it would be quite exciting, and it would also be fascinating if Jesus Christ returned, although I have a horrible feeling if he did, he would be diagnosed as schizophrenic and locked away in Broadmoor for making so much trouble. But neither of these metaphors really strikes me very much as a symbol for what is coming. I am more convinced and much more awestruck by the process which takes place in individuals.

Audience: I've recently read something about the Hindu idea of the Kali Yuga and the cycle of creation and destruction. According to their thinking, we are heading toward the destruction phase of the cosmic process.

Liz: Yes, I have encountered this idea of the Kali Yuga. I think it is another great mythic interpretation of a symbol. In the Middle Ages people were very fond of thinking of the world in similar terms, the idea that there was once a Golden Age and then men began to become corrupt and deteriorate and eventually there will be destruction by fire or water and the Golden Age will return. The idea that history is cyclical on a grand scale, that God breathes in and out and creation manifests and unmanifests is a very ancient idea. I am once again inclined to take these things as imaginal interpretations of a basic psychic process which describes the development of consciousness. One can take this theme of the Golden Age very individually, as an archetypal experience of the bliss of union with Mother-God in the womb. Birth is like a Fall, an entry into darkness and corruption and mortality. As the ego develops it becomes increasingly separate and isolated and alone, until the sense of alienation becomes almost unbearable and the fantasies arise spontaneously about the blissful past which also becomes the blissful future when one will be reunited with the source in death or in paradise.

That may sound horribly reductive and psychological to some of you, but there is nothing reductive about an archetypal experience. Whether we speak of the experience of the soul on its own plane before incarnation, or of the unity of the unconscious of mother and child in the womb, the experience is a numinous one and we are forever trying to find it again. In a sense this expulsion from paradise, from the unconscious, is also true historically. There is a movement out of the *participation mystique* and the unconsciousness of the primitive, toward what we call civilisation and the development of the conscious ego. Anthropology bears out the myth of the Golden Age in terms of the development of individual and tribal consciousness. The only cure for too much corruption is a death, an ending, and then a rebirth. I think there is an equation of unconsciousness with innocence, and of consciousness with corruption. In a sense, Prometheus' fire is the same as Adam's bite of the apple. It is a sin against Mother Nature.

This is one of the themes in Goethe's *Faust*. The great sin is the tampering with nature, because the moment we tamper and rob the unconscious of its treasure in order to build up the ego, we are stealing something from God. And God is very jealous of that treasure. This is also the mythic theme of the dragon fight, to retrieve the treasure that the dragon guards. Siegfried does this in Wagner's *Ring*, and so do a hundred Greek and Teutonic and Celtic and Indian heroes. In the Garden of Eden, God is very jealous of the Tree of Good and Evil, and even more jealous of the Tree of Life. The fruits of these trees would make man God, and God fights back in the same way that the unconscious fights back when one tries to bring anything into consciousness. Yet that same unconscious paradoxically encourages the process, just as God paradoxically has created Adam with the will to make his choice.

So the Fall is a symbol of man's corruption and descent, or ascent, depending on how you look at it, into consciousness. The only resolution for deepening corruption is some kind of cyclical return to the source, a cleansing or baptism by water or fire, so that there can be a reuniting of the two severed parts. The destruction of creation is also a renewal of creation, a return to the Father or the Mother.

Audience: The myth of the Garden of Eden was originally Sumerian, and the serpent wasn't a symbol of evil.

Liz: Yes, I am familiar with that. But the collective has chosen to remember it in another way, and it is what the myth has meant to us for so many centuries that I think is relevant. Because we seem to contain an innate guilt for the development of human consciousness, we look back over our shoulders and feel we have sinned. Whether the myth was changed or misinterpreted is interesting but in a sense irrelevant, because the myth which is alive for us in the West is the myth of Adam's fall. Perhaps the Sumerians felt less guilt about consciousness. Or maybe they were typical of ancient cultures, and were not far removed from the unconscious, so there was not so much awareness of a loss and a Fall. I have a feeling that this underlying, archetypal guilt is one of the reasons why we must justify our psychological tampering with illness. We only really look within if we are driven to it, not if we are left alone. Any descent into the unconscious psyche is a loss of innocence. It is particularly hard on innocence because one discovers that the gods themselves are muddled and in need of transformation, and that is gross heresy in terms of Western religious tradition. The worst corruption, which the alchemists were steeped in, is the shocking recognition that God is not yet conscious and may need a little help. But rather than face what this might mean, we project our corruption onto the world outside and look at our monetary system and our technology and say, "Oh, how corrupt and sinful and disgusting." Then we have millenarian visions of the end of the world and the return to the Golden Age, or we try to go back to nature to recapture our innocence by eating wholemeal bread, just as Marie Antoinette used to dress up as a shepherdess and play with lambs and goats in the gardens of Versailles in order to escape her corruption and get back to the Golden Age again.

This seems to be a deep collective vision in us all, the belief that once we were innocent and lived in harmony with God and nature, and now we are corrupt and have lost our souls. The problem is how to make the return without the destruction of all that we have built. The Tarot describes this circle of innocence descending into corruption and returning to innocence again in a very beautiful way. The Fool begins the cycle of the Trumps, and he is innocent. He is in a state of unconsciousness at the beginning.

He travels through the different paths reflected by the other Trumps, passing through Death and the Devil and his redemption in the Hanged Man. At the end of the cycle we are back to the Fool again, who has no number on his card, because he is at the beginning and the end of the journey.

Audience: Is innocence unconscious or instinctual?

Liz: That's a very difficult question. No one seems to be very clear about just what is meant by instinct. Certainly instincts are unconscious, in the sense that they are not contrived by the ego but exist as a life-support system within every living organism, within the flesh itself. In that sense they are innocent. The very potent fantasy of the "natural" man which fascinated Gauguin and D. H. Lawrence so much is a vision of the divine innocence of the instincts. One of the most omnipresent symbols of this divine innocence is the image of the child, the divine child. The child lives from his centre, from his Self, from his instincts, but he also represents the potential for new consciousness. We project this inner experience of divine, childlike innocence on our actual children, who may not be in the least innocent and certainly carry inherent predispositions of character which make them individuals. But we like to believe that children are innocent blank slates, because we project this vision of the divine child upon them. Children can be horribly cruel and quite violent, as Melanie Klein writes about so well. But the divine child is the embodiment of innocence, the thing that existed before the ego became alienated from the instincts and from the unconscious.

Audience: In Eastern teaching the world and its corruption are only illusion anyway, and the reality is the state of oneness with God.

Liz: Well, I can't argue with that, can I? No doubt somewhere the soul is dreaming and what we think is life is really its dream. This is also the Hindu idea of the Kali Yuga. Brahma breathes in and the manifest universe disappears. Brahma breathes out and the manifest universe comes into being. I'm sure at the moment that Brahma is writhing in his sleep, having a bad dream. I'm not really in a position to say what is Truth and what is Reality. I haven't the foggiest idea. But one of the things I have been trying to communicate to you during the course of the weekend is that the end of the world is an archetypal theme and describes an inner process, and that it might be very helpful and relevant to us all if we could learn to distinguish a symbol from a concrete prognostication of doom. The millenarian myth is a cyclical myth, and has a tendency to erupt at regular intervals from the collective psyche at points of great change. If we don't make the effort to understand what might be trying to emerge on an inner level, then we compel the myth to actualise in the most concrete form, and then we really will have the end of the world, because we possess the technology to bring it about.

Obviously something is happening to us all. Each person's perception of it is coloured by his own psychic constitution, his own dreams and aspirations and visions and insecurities and fears and parents and ideologies. I have yet to be convinced of such a thing as complete objectivity. Perhaps all one can do is be conscious of where the individual ends and the collective begins, and to be aware of the mythic element in our terror of holocaust. This is a time of immense mythic blossoming, although you wouldn't think it if you turned on the television. But the dawn of a new astrological age always releases new myths. These themes are all around us, and astrologers are particularly subjected to them—the end of the world, the return of the Golden Age, the vengeance of God, the cleansing of sins. So I think it is a wise idea to remember these things when next someone asks you in terror if the Uranus-Neptune-Saturn conjunction means the end of the world. The way we feel about these things reflects our own individual capacity to cope with the changes that are around and inside us. Blind fatalism of a negative kind and blind fatalism of a positive kind are both ways of avoiding the very difficult and ambivalent place in the middle, where there might be some choice but where the choice ultimately depends upon individual responsibility. I wish I had answers but I am afraid I am much too preoccupied with trying to find some for my own life.

Audience: Can you recommend any reading material on these themes?

Liz: Yes, a good place to begin might be Norman Cohn's book, *The Pursuit of the Millenium.* He is concerned with the outbreaks of millenarian spirit during the Middle Ages, but he is drawing obvious conclusions about the present as well. He's also written a book called *Europe's Inner Demons* which is extremely interesting. It's about the witch hunts of the sixteenth and seventeenth centuries, but once again he draws parallels with the psychology of the twentieth century. Obviously anything of Jung's is relevant, particularly *The Archetypes and the Collective Unconscious* (Volume 9 of the *Collected Works*, Part 1) and *Aion* (Volume 9, Part 2). *Psychology and Alchemy* (Volume 12) is a wonderful book. If you're interested in the theme of the Golden Age, you might try Harry Levin's book, *The Myth of the Golden Age in the Renaissance*. I can't really think at the moment of any others, although history and mythology and depth psychology I think ought to be requisite reading for any astrologer wanting to understand the outer planets and the collective.

Audience: Would you be willing to run through the outer planets in aspect to the inner ones, just giving a brief interpretation, or would that be too boring for you?

Liz: It's not a question of boredom, it's just not really the way I like to teach. I think it would be lovely if you, since you asked, could sit down and put together a good "cookbook" of interpretations of this kind. These kinds of books are immensely useful to the astrology student and I've always found them very valuable. But I suppose what I would hope is that you can get the gist of how to work with the outer planets and go home and do some thinking for yourself. I would not like to quote cookbook interpretations and have you parrot them. I would much rather see you struggle to put something together in your own words from a basic idea or inspiration that you might get from the weekend. I would hate to think that anybody has just copied and memorised anything I've said. That would be horrible, my words coming out of your mouth. I would rather feel that I have succeeded in communicating something of the core of the meaning of the outer planets, so that you can compile your own list of aspects. Throughout the weekend I have been talking about this problem of finding out what things might mean to oneself individually. How do you feel the outer planets work in your own chart? What can you put together yourself? I hope you can understand why I can't teach like that. But if you write a cookbook of outer planet aspects yourself, I promise I'll buy it.